D0886722

Imaginary
Apparatus

Imaginary Apparatus

New York City and and Its Mediated Representation

McLain Clutter

 PARK BOOKS

For Denis McMillan Clutter

Contents

Introduction

New York City's mediatic emanations are multiple and ubiquitous, flowing through celluloid, pixel, and neuron with sublime complexity.[1] The production, dissemination, and consumption of the city's mediated self composes a vast, swirling and dynamic media ecology—analogous, in a sense, to the equally sublime ecology of the city itself, its systemic interconnections between built form, flow, population, environment, economics, subjective affect, and more.[2] This is a book about the manifold relationship *between* these two complex objects of sublimity, between New York City and its mediated representation. Today, it is perhaps a truism that one's experience of urbanism is always intertwined with expectations conditioned by media. Indeed, mediated representations of our cities saturate every corner of urban life. But this apparent second-nature of the contemporary city is in fact *naturalized*, the summary effect of identifiable actors, political and economic interests, and pervasive cultural sensibilities. This book forwards a partial history of that naturalization by tracing one series of developments through which New York City and its mediated representation became intertwined.

Cities have often been theorized as the material locales for collectivity. From the ancient Greek agora in which citizens assembled for debate, to the intricate public interactions on Jane Jacob's

---

1　Here, I allude to recent thought on the nature of images, and their motions through medium and mind, most prominently developed by Hans Belting. See Hans Belting, *An Anthropology of Images: Picture, Medium, Body* (Princeton: Princeton University Press, 2011).

2　The phrase "media ecology" is used here to indicate the iterative flow of media between mediums and audiences, and the feedback that might affect media production and audience perception

at every point along such a discourse. While the precise understanding of the phrase used here is borne out in the arguments that follow, the phrase is sometimes attributed to Neil Postman, and draws on the ideas of Marshall McLuhan, Walter Ong, and others. See Casey Man Kong Lum, ed., *Perspectives on Culture, Technology, and Communication: The Media Ecology Tradition* (Cresskill, NJ: Hampton Press, 2006), 1–60.

Greenwich Village sidewalk, the space of the city has been conceptualized as the milieu in which the public is consolidated.[3] Within this paradigm, architecture plays a critical role. Buildings *define* the space of common experience. Monuments and institutional structures *represent* the urban public.[4] But this role historically granted to the city and its architecture has long been complicated by the emergence of contemporary media culture.[5] The circulation of media, its images and effects, now provide an alternate register of common experience. Mediated images of cities now compete with their material referent to be loci of collective association.

In the analyses that follow, mediated representations of urbanism—images, films, photographs, and more—assume heightened agency. So much more than mere registrations of apparent reality, or even projections of visionary futures, urban representations are here understood to be both instrumental and ideological, operating on their audiences in ways ranging from the affective to the communicative. Indeed, mediated representations of urbanism can *represent* the public, condition expectation of urban life, and frame common experience. However, the intention here is not to outstrip the agency of the architect or urban designer. To the contrary, what follows is meant to

3   For one account of the role of the agora in the ancient Greek Polis, see Lewis Mumford, *The City in History: Its Origins, Its Transformations, and Its Prospects* (New York: Harcourt, Brace & World, 1961), 148–150.
     Jane Jacobs, *The Death and Life of Great American Cities* (New York: Modern Library, 1969), 55–73.
4   Among the most thorough theorizations of the representational capacities of architecture and the role of architecture in structuring the reality of the city has been that by Aldo Rossi. See Aldo Rossi, *The Architecture of the City* (Cambridge: MIT Press, 1984).
5   Among many others, Paul Virilio has made this point, writing "From the town as theatre of human activity with its church square and market place

bustling with so many present actors and spectators, to CINECITTA and then TELECITTA, bustling with absent televiewers, it was just a short step through that venerable urban invention, the shop window. This putting behind glass of objects and people, the implementation of a transparency that has intensified over the past few decades, has led, beyond the optics of photography and cinema, to an optoelectronics of the means of television broadcasting. These are now capable of creating not only window-apartments and houses, but window-towns window-nations, media megacities that have the paradoxical power of bringing individuals together long-distance, around standardized opinions and behaviors." Paul Virilio, *The Vision Machine* (Bloomington: Indiana University Press, 1994), 65.

describe an expanded field of operation for these disciplines. This book meets its audience at a time when those who might design future urbanisms have at their hands technologies for imaging their ideation in far greater virtuosity and quantity than ever before. And yet the effects of these representations, how they affect their audiences and through them the city, seem vagrantly underexplored. What follows recites a method through which the contemporary designer might conceptualize the agency or entrapments of the urban representations she creates. In this book, the physical reality of New York City, its images and their attendant narratives, associations, and even memories, are understood to be alike as malleable participants in the complex processes through which the city is defined.

In so many ways, the ambitions of this book are far too large for any single volume.[6] The circulation of mediated representations of our cities is thoroughly pervasive; the task of unpacking how such mediation effects, precedes and intermingles with material reality is intractable. Performing such an analysis of New York, among the most common cities appearing in all manner of media, seems doubly a fool's errand. The task is predisposed to naïve conclusions and vagrant generalizations. There is no *single* relationship between

6 To this point, a substantial body of scholarly and consumer oriented literature about New York's appearance in media precedes this volume. Most prominent are those discussing film and the city. Several existing studies address the history of the film industry in New York, categorize tropes of urban representation that are recurrent in media produced in the city, or offer analyses of the cultural narratives or aesthetic sensibilities embedded within New York City films of varying genre or era. See, for example, David I. Grossvogel, *Scenes in the City: Film Visions of Manhattan Before 9/11* (New York: Peter Lang Publishing, 2003); Richard A. Blake, *Street Smart: The New York of Lumet, Allen, Scorsese, and Lee* (Lexington: University of Kentucky Press, 2005); Stanley Corkin, *Starring New York: Filming the Grime and the Glamour of the Long 1970's* (New York: Oxford University Press, 2011). See also my previous essay: McLain Clutter, "Imaginary Apparatus: Film Production and Urban Planning in New York City, 1966–1973," *Grey Room 35* (Spring 2009), pp. 55–89. Distinct from most previous work, the present volume aspires to describe the instrumental nature of various media representations, and conceptualizations of urbanism that seem affected by media, or planning and urban design practices that have profoundly impacted New York's material environment. In doing so, this book also addresses political, economic, and social factors related to New York's mediated representation that received little attention in prior literature.

New York and its mediated representation. Indeed, there is no *single* mediated image of New York City to analyze.

Accordingly, I have limited the scope of this analysis. This book begins with a focus on developments occurring in a short period in New York City's history, from 1966 to 1973. I then offer architectural and urban analyses of New York's built environment that are best understood in relation to the crucible of historical context I provide. The years bracketing the core of my investigation coincide with the mayoral tenure of John V. Lindsay.[7] This era also coincides with what is commonly termed the "urban crisis" in American cities. During these years, cities nationwide sustained the effects of profound economic restructuring, transitioning from industrial to post-industrial economic bases, while experiencing an out-migration of the urban middle class. Simultaneously, urban space became the locale for cultural revolution and mounting social and racial unrest. In New York, the immediate effects of these phenomena included labor strikes, divisive racial sentiments, and a depleting municipal tax base that culminated with the city's fiscal crisis of 1975.[8] Meanwhile, institutionalized methods of urban planning were being challenged at the grass-roots level by the

7   In doing so, this book joins others in documenting the history of media, architecture, and urban development in New York during the Lindsay Administration. See, for example, Robert A.M. Stern, Thomas Mellins and David Fishman, *New York 1960: architecture and urbanism between the Second World War and the Bicentennial* (New York: Monacelli Press, 1995), 1174–1199; James Sanders, *Celluloid Skyline: New York and the Movies* (New York: Alfred A. Knopf, 2003), 343–442; Stanley Corkin, *Starring New York: Filming the Grime and the Glamour of the Long 1970's* (New York: Oxford University Press, 2011). More recently, a surge of interest in John Lindsay has produced a documentary entitled *The Lindsay Years*, which first aired in 2010 on the WNET public television station in New York, a 2010 exhibit at the City Museum of New York curated by Steven

H. Jaffe entitled *America's Mayor: John V. Lindsay and the Reinvention of New York*, and a book of essays of the same name. See Sam Roberts, ed., *America's Mayor: John V. Lindsay and the Reinvention of New York* (New York: Columbia University Press, 2010). Also of note is David Gissen's recent book on the emergence of interior urban environments in New York City across a time period that intersects with the Lindsay Administration. See David Gissen, *Manhattan Atmospheres: Architecture, The Interior Environment, and Urban Crisis* (Minneapolis: University of Minnesota Press, 2014).

8   David Harvey, "Flexible Accumulation through Urbanization Reflections on 'Post-Modernism' in the American City," *Perspecta*, vol. 26, Theater, Theatricality, and Architecture (1990), 255.

urban populace. The years prior to Lindsay's tenure saw the application of European modernist planning principles in the form of urban renewal, and intense investment in automotive infrastructure, reflecting the strong hand of Robert Moses in shaping New York City's built environment. When Lindsay took office he met an urban public that was newly mobilized against Moses-era planning principles and the top-down governmental model of which they were emblematic.[9]

Against this tumultuous setting, and seemingly tangential to the city's most pressing concerns, the Lindsay Administration initiated an unprecedented effort to draw on-location media production to New York's streets. Simultaneously, Lindsay's Planning Commission drafted a series of documents that, sometimes unintentionally, reflect conceptual and aesthetic influences of various visual media. The contention here is that the effects of these two areas of activity under Lindsay were richly interrelated. This commingling of media production policy and urban planning then proved resonant with contemporaneous business developments in film and television production, and emergent cultural attitudes towards media. This book describes a relationship between New York City and its mediated representation at the conjuncture of these policies and circumstances— tracing the interrelation of their attendant cultural, economic and aesthetic valences. Thus, this book unpacks one story of the conditions through which New York's mediated representation became imbricated within the city's physical reality,

9   For a concise account of these developments in New York see, Sam Roberts, "City in Crisis I," in America's Mayor: John V. Lindsay and the Reinvention of New York, ed. Sam Roberts (New York: Columbia University Press, 2010) 10–25, and Steven Weisman, "City in Crisis II," in America's Mayor: John V. Lindsay and the Reinvention of New York, ed. Sam Roberts (New York: Columbia University Press, 2010), 192–213.

and identifies evidence of this effect within the built environment.

In a sense, the conclusions to this book are foregone. The relationship between mediated representations and cities is a well-trod area of inquiry. Certainly among the most recurrent positions in this field is one that condemns the corrosive effects of media on cities. Long before the emergence of the present vast array of media forms, from film to television to youtube, cultural critics were issuing cautionary narratives as to the persistence of the physical reality of cities in a media culture, and the ideological associations such mediation might project on urbanism. In his 1926 book, *The Culture of Cities*, Louis Mumford derided the environment of the early twentieth-century metropolis as a "shadow world" of paper and celluloid. He asserted that social interactions within the urban environment were increasingly "framed for their effect on paper; or they are posed, with a view to historic reproduction, in the photograph or the motion picture."[10] Palpable within Mumford's words is a lament for a bygone, directly lived urbanism that had been rendered inaccessible through the obfuscation of mediated representation. It seemed as if the physical city could no longer be occupied as such; instead, city streets and squares alike were understood to be tantamount to scenographic backdrops, in anticipation of eventual media dissemination. The urban public, in this scenario, become actors in a physical reality that has been rendered effuse with the character of the virtual. Prevalent throughout the twentieth century, this line of thought perhaps found its summit as it became more ideologically charged under

[10] Louis Mumford, *The Culture of Cities* (New York: Harcourt, Brace and Company, 1938), 256.

the moniker *spectacle*, an idea most prominently developed by the French Marxist theorist Guy Debord, in his 1967 manifesto *The Society of the Spectacle*.

Debord defined spectacle as a condition wherein the societal misrecognition of reality that is a central tenant of classic Marxism is deeply mediated through the visual world of appearances.[11] Thus, Debord's often quoted aphorism, "All that once was directly lived has become mere representation."[12] The theorist argued that within the condition of spectacle, the subject is alienated from the material world—and the embedded social relations with which Marxism charges the material—by a layer of visuality whose intoxicating seductions mystify social reality and uphold the dominant regime of capital accumulation. Debord extolled: "The spectacle is not a collection of images; rather, it is a social relationship between people that is mediated by images."[13] Recalling the early laments of Mumford and others, for Debord the proliferation of media-generated representations stood between the subject and direct experience of the physical world as such. Writing in France in the 1960s, the historical context for Debord's work is not dissimilar from that of the present volume: transformative urban deindustrialization, emergent social unrest, and the recent ubiquity of mass media in formats ranging from the magazine to the household television.

11   By this, I refer to the Marxist concept of ideology, of false consciousness, in which the proletariat subject is unaware of the exploitation and subordination that is systematically imposed upon him or her by capitalism. In classic Marxism, such exploitation and subordination is embedded in social relationships that are mediated by commodities. In Debord's conceptualization of spectacle, the mystifying capacities of the commodity are largely assumed by representations. The proletariat subject subscribes to dubious representations of his or her social condition that describe a false reality, alienate the subject from the material world, and imbue *false consciousness*.

12   Guy Debord, *The Society of the Spectacle* (New York: Zone Books, 1995), 1.

13   Debord, 3.

Debord's thoughts are recalled by the later work of numerous critics and theorists specifically addressing the 20th century American city. To many, American cities evinced a spectral character, wherein the visual impression of urbanism assumed new prominence and heightened capacities for the mystification of physical reality. Jean Baudrillard famously remarked, "The American city seems to have stepped right out of the movies." Thus, in order to understand urbanism within the United States one must "begin with the screen and move outwards to the city."[14] Similarly, Michael Sorkin has described Disneyland as a model for postmodern American urbanism in which "the ephemeral reality of the cinema is concretized into the stuff of the city."[15] Sorkin laments this "urbanism for the electronic age" as a capitalist utopia that provokes subjective estrangement and geographic sameness.[16]

Indeed, Baudrillard, Sorkin and others were addressing the visual character of the American city in the wake of the profound political and economic restructuring of the urban landscape that was imminent precisely as Debord extolled the spectacle, and as the events discussed in this book were unfolding. As the industrial economies of American cities faded, employment in service and office labor surged throughout the later decades of the twentieth century. Cities became primarily centers of immaterial production. Urban geographies were modified to attract international investment, and the entertainment and tourist revenues of the upwardly mobile gentry and the

14 Jean Baudrillard, *America*, trans. Chris Turner (New York: Verso, 1989), 56.

15 Michael Sorkin, "See You in Disneyland," in *Variations on a Theme Park* (New York: Hill and Wang, 1992), 227.

16 Sorkin, 232.

suburban middle class. In this new paradigm, urban representations were essential tools in the
popularization of a city's renewed image, fueling
subsequent gentrification. Combined with economic deregulation and the increased privatizing
of civic services, these developments constitute
the neoliberal city as theorized by David Harvey,
Saskia Sassen, Neil Smith, and others.[17]

In her book *The City of Collective Memory: Its
Historic Imagery and Architectural Entertainments*,
Christine Boyer addresses the role of spectacle
and mediation in neoliberal urban development
through subject matter most germane to the present volume. First published in 1994, Boyer's book
was written at the twilight of the architectural style
of postmodernism, a movement that often produced urban design of a historicist, pictorial, or
imagistic character. Such designs were meant to
reconnect to narrative, history, or a sensibility
more populist than the totalizing urban reforma-
tions characteristic of modernism and institutionalized urban renewal.[18] In Boyer's assessment,
postmodern urban design was problematic in its
reticence towards holistic designs for cities, thus
abandoning the social and utopian goals of modernism. Instead postmodern architects and urban
designers sought to develop the city at a piece-
meal and localized scale that was far too susceptible to the corrosive influence of capital and private
interests. And the historicist style of postmodernism fell victim to the same, forwarding an aesthetic

17   See, for example, David Harvey, *The Condition
      of Postmodernity: An Enquiry in to the Origins
      of Cultural Change* (Oxford: Blackwell, 1989);
      Saskia Sassen, *The Global City* (Princeton, N.J.:
      Princeton University Press, 1991); Neil Smith, *The
      New Urban Frontier: Gentrification and the Re-
      vanchist City* (London: Routledge, 1996).
18   David Harvey has provided a concise definition of
      postmodernism as it affected the urban environ-
      ment, noting: "In the urban context, therefore,

      I shall simply characterize post-modernism as
      signifying a break with the idea that planning
      and development should focus on large-scale,
      technologically rational, austere and function-
      ally efficient 'international style' design, and that
      vernacular traditions, local history, and special-
      ized spatial designs ranging from functions of in-
      timacy to grand spectacle should be approached
      with a much greater eclecticism of style." Harvey,
      The Condition of Postmodernity, 66.

featuring historic architectural quotations and visual codes that, divorced from their original contexts, intoxicated the urban public with nostalgic
sentiments working in the interest of private capital accumulation, and obscuring the possibility of
a critical cultural consciousness. Again recalling
Debord, Boyer nominated the urban milieu of postmodern architecture "The City of Spectacle," a context in which the prevalence of fragmentary urban
representations circulating through all manner of
visual media worked to further estrange meaningful historic context, amplifying the possibility of
ideological mystification.[19]

Important to this book, Boyer dwells on two
major New York City projects from the 1980s as
instances of development within the visual regime
of spectacle, the redevelopment of the South Street
Seaport and the expansion of lower Manhattan
westward into Battery Park City. Writing about
the transformation of the South Street Seaport
from a dilapidated working dock to a tourist attraction, Boyer argues: "A new visuality is introduced into the cityscape by reducing the language
of architecture to a serial experimentation with
pure signs, media codes, styles, or fashions."[20]
True to her thesis, Boyer contends that the historic stage-set redevelopment of the Seaport had
been executed through the deployment of a tab-
leau of solipsistic urban representations that were
conditioned by, and circulated through, visual
media. In doing so, architects and developers have
implemented scenographic historic quotations

19   In *The City of Collective Memory*, Boyer compel-
     lingly describes a lineage of pictorial representa-
     tional regimes in western city design, harkening
     to framed urban vistas characteristic of what she
     called "The City as a Work of Art" in 19th century
     Paris, proceeding to "The City as Panorama" with
     the mobility of the early 20th century metropolis,

     and culminating with the then-contemporary
     "City of Spectacle," the milieu of postmodern ar-
     chitecture. Christine Boyer, *The City of Collective
     Memory: Its Historical Imagery and Architectural
     Entertainments* (Cambridge: MIT Press, 1994),
     33–59.

20   Boyer, 426.

and visual codes that benefit only the interests of private capital accumulation, while complying with a paradigm of urban development devoid of critical or utopian ambitions. Boyer's alternative is a city built of eclectic and disjunctive imagery from collective memory, which existed prior to the misrecognition of the past imposed by codified history and spectacle. Collective memory, Boyer argues, remains latent in the everyday spaces of the city, awaiting excavation.[21]

Boyer's critique is sound, as are those of Sorkin, Harvey, Smith and so many others who have, with varying degrees of condemnation, described the insidious capacities of spectacle and mediated representation in neoliberal urbanization. Certainly, imagery conditioned through media imposes on our cities contentious ideological alliances—disguising consumer space as classically conceived public space, writing into the visuality of the built environment constructed narratives that paper-over difference, and more. And yet, in condemning the effects of mediated imagery on the urban environment, one is susceptible to naïve assumptions of a more authentic urban condition that lies just below the intoxicating visual layer of spectacular mystification. It is enticing to believe that such an original condition existed prior to spectacle, perhaps awaiting social action or design techniques that might awaken the urban subject and grant her access to a more directly lived urbanity. This book is written in the spirit of deep skepticism towards such narratives of urban authenticity.[22] Indeed, the seductions of similar narratives are

21   Boyer, 48.
22   Such suspicion aligns with Slavoj Zizek's remarks that "... the main point is to see how reality itself cannot reproduce itself without so-called ideological mystification. The mask (*of spectacle, of* *ideology*) is not simply hiding the real state of things; the ideological distortion is written into its very essence." Slavoj Zizek, *The Sublime Object of Ideology* (New York: Verso, 1989), 28.

responsible for precisely the deployment of histor-ical urban imagery that Boyer and others have found contentious. The argument here is that the material reality of the contemporary city, and New York in particular, is simply far too inter-twined with its mediated representations for any revelation of a pre-spectacular condition.[23] Medi-ated representations of cities are so pervasive and interconnected with the apparent reality of ur-banism that they have thoroughly colonized the very subjective memories that some might deem revelatory.[24]

The above concession isn't granted as an act of complicity with spectacle, nor to cede the visu-ality of our cities strictly to the interests of capital. Rather, this book concedes the intractable satura-tion of spectacle in order to signal a change in strat-egy. The hope here is that by better understanding the mechanics through which urban reality is in-termeshed with mediated representation, new tac-tics for operating on the city may be enabled. In this scenario, visual media may be an ally, and not a hindrance. One might operate on the city *through* its mediated representation.

Such an understanding of the potentially re-demptive capacities of visual media for the urban environment is also not new. Most often, interest in the topic builds upon early twentieth-century theorization of the structural commonality be-tween cinema and the metropolis. Canonical texts by Georg Simmel and Walter Benjamin are often

23   The suspicion here, also, is that a "pre-spectacu-lar" condition may never have existed in New York. Urban histories such as Max Page's *The Creative Destruction of Manhattan* 1900–1940 (Chicago: University of Chicago Press, 1999) and William R. Taylor's *In Pursuit of Gotham* (London: Oxford University Press, 1992) convincingly demon-strate that the mode of urban development that Boyer labels "spectacular" is far from a recent applique to New York's urban environment, but a

tradition beginning early in New York's emergence as a major metropolis.

24   Boyer concedes this fact. She wrote: "By now, tra-ditions have been so thoroughly 'invented' or ho-mogenized, and 'history' so absolutely marketed or commodified, misrepresented, or rendered in-visible, that any oppositional potential rooted in collective memory has been eclipsed complete-ly." Boyer, 5.

drawn upon to assert the synergy between the
ability of the film camera to capture motion, and
the new and unprecedented kinesis of the capitalist metropolis.[25] Thus, the registration of urban
dynamics on film became an analogue for understanding the registration of stimuli on the consciousness of the urban subject. Benjamin elaborated on these ideas. Working in a Marxist
tradition, the theorist suggested that because of
cinema's privileged capacity to represent the metropolis, it might awaken the viewing subject from
ideological misrecognition of urban reality.[26] Similarly, but decades later, Siegfried Kracauer asserted that cinema's realist capacities had the ability
to reintroduce obdurate material reality to a society that had lapsed into abstraction.[27] For both of
these theorists, cinema became a vehicle through
which urban reality could be re-seen, thus motivat-
ing social progress among a newly conscious urban
public.

This book will draw upon ideas first forwarded by Simmel, Benjamin, Kracauer, and others.
Despite divergent historical contexts, several visual media discussed here maintain a privilege in
re-presenting the physical reality of New York City
during the Lindsay Administration in ways that
recall observations by these theorists of early modernity. However, such facile formal observations,

25   See Walter Benjamin, "The Work of Art in the Age
      of Mechanical Reproduction," in *Illuminations*
      (New York: Shocken Books, 1968), 217–251 and
      Georg Simmel, "The Metropolis and Mental Life,"
      in *The Sociology of Georg Simmel*, adapt. D.
      Weinstein, trans. Kurt Wolff (New York: Free Press,
      1950), 409–424.

26   Benjamin believed in the revolutionary capacity
      of the medium "in permitting the reproduction to
      meet the beholder or listener in his own particular
      situation" to "reactivate the object reproduced,"
      hence awakening the viewing subject from dis-
      traction and ideology. Benjamin, "Work of Art,"
      221.

27   In his 1960 book *Theory of Film: The Redemption
      of Physical Reality* (New York: Oxford University
      Press, 1965), Kracauer situates society in a state
      of abstraction bereft of the bygone unifying belief
      structures. Echoing Benjamin, Kracauer grants
      cinema an intrinsic ability to awaken audience
      consciousness of reality, hence countering soci-
      etal abstraction with the reintroduced *material*.
      For Kracauer, this was not really an awakening
      from ideology. He claimed that societal abstrac-
      tion had made the conditions of the time post-
      ideological. Rather, cinema could reintroduce to
      consciousness the material realities that were,
      then, newly available in the wake of ideology's dis-
      integration (287–296).

taken alone, give way to generalizations—ignoring critical incongruities between the formal, social and political conditions of each city and each system of media production. A more heterogeneous approach is required to trace the relationship between New York and its mediated representation of interest here.

This investigation cast a broad net. Aesthetic and formal analysis is one of several registers within a discourse that is also inclusive of urban policy and economics, business developments in the media production industries, and the subjectivities that all of these interests implicate. In weaving my analysis through such heterogeneity, this book traces connections that are often latent, partial, or fleeting. The analysis eschews disciplinary pieties and media specificities in ways that may draw criticism from academics from an array of fields. Such a method has not been applied in solicitation of criticism, but because the relationship between New York and its mediated representation of concern here is only visible when a broad ecology of interests are allowed to liberally establish interconnections and alliances. Rem Koolhaas's characterization of the Paranoid-Critical Method as "the compression of (these) gaseous speculations to a critical point where they achieve the density of fact" is perhaps a methodological cousin.[28] More precisely, the concept of the *apparatus* has provided methodological guidance. The apparatus has been developed in two related theoretical trajectories—one building upon the work of Michel Foucault and a second trajectory in media studies, including contributions by Jean-Louis Baudry, Christian Metz, and others.

28   Rem Koolhaas, *Delirious New York* (New York: Monacelli Press, 1994), 238.

Distinct from the colloquial use of the word, the Foucaultian apparatus—the French *dispositif*—is not a mere device. Rather, it is an assemblage of actors, ideas, objects, and more that performs a structural or organizational role in the bracketing of the knowable and the maintenance of power. Foucault understood apparatuses to both produce subjectivities, and enroll the participation of those subjects within their systems of relation. While never precisely defining the term, Foucault came closest to distilling his sense of the word apparatus in a 1977 interview. The theorist explained:

> (an apparatus) is, firstly, a thoroughly heterogeneous ensemble consisting of discourses, institutions, architectural forms, regulatory decisions, laws, administrative measures, scientific statements, philosophical, moral and philanthropic propositions—in short, the said as much as the unsaid. Such are the elements of the apparatus. The apparatus itself is the system of relations that can be established between these elements.[29]

Hence, for Foucault, the apparatus was a conceptual construct for explaining the complex and instrumentalized network of relationships between elements of disparate categories. Understood as participants in an apparatus, physical artifacts, legal proceedings, philosophical traditions, technological developments and more—each of which could be subject to discrete analysis under the terms of its own disciplinary ontology—can be understood as nodes within a network of forces and relationships. Critically, it is the underlying network or system itself that is indicated by the

29   Michel Foucault, "The Confession of the Flesh," in
      *Power/Knowledge: Selected Interviews and
      Other Writings 1972–1977*, ed. Colin Gordon (New
      York: Pantheon Books, 1980), 194.

Foucaultian sense of the term *apparatus*. The concept of the Foucaultian apparatus has been instructive here in discerning the complex network of relationships between policy and design during the Lindsay Administration, and seemingly unrelated developments in the media industries and urban culture at large.

Foucault further described the conditions in which one might expect an apparatus to emerge—times of crisis or instability. In these contexts, the development of an apparatus serves to secure the dominant regime of power and knowledge. He wrote:

> Thirdly, I understand by the term 'apparatus' a sort of—shall we say formation which has as its major function at a given historical moment that of responding to an urgent need. The apparatus thus has a dominant strategic function.[30]

Foucault's forecast aligns compellingly with the historical context provided in this book. Combined with the fiscal, social, and physical crises prevalent within New York during the Lindsay Administration, the Mayor's tenure coincided with a period of instability in the media industries. Most notably, the burgeoning ubiquity of television within every American home threatened the stalwart Hollywood film industry. Responding to this crisis, the major Hollywood studios restructured their production models in ways that were complimentary with Lindsay's attempts to draw media production to New York. This book provides a broad analysis of the conjuncture of actions by the Lindsay Administration and the media industries within the period of inquiry here—a period of crisis and instability for each, and fertile ground for the emergence of a Foucaultian apparatus.[31]

Contemporary to Foucault's development of the apparatus, a related sense of the term was emerging in film criticism, as theorists were becoming concerned with the role of institutional interests, economics, and the related psychic resonance of film among spectators in determining Hollywood production. The most influential group of theorists with these interests was formed around the French film journal *Cahiers du Cinema*, and included Jean-Louis Baudry, Jean-Louis Comolli, and Christian Metz. Drawing heavily from the Marxism of Louis Althusser and the psychoanalytic theory of Jacques Lacan, their ideas came to be known as apparatus theory.[32]

Central to the apparatus theory of film is the concept of the cinematic institution. Through repeated cinema attendance, the cinematic institution imposes upon spectators an orientation of consciousness toward the consumption of the products of the film industry.[33] Those who watch cinema are conditioned to negotiate their subjectivities in relation to the images on the movie screen. Theories of the cinematic institution often

31   In recent years, the philosopher Giorgio Agamben has been instrumental in vivifying the importance of the Foucaultian apparatus, both in regards to Foucault's own work, and for contemporary culture at large. See Giorgio Agamben, *What Is An Apparatus? and Other Essays* (Stanford, California: Stanford University Press, 2009), 1–24. Referring to the "boundless growth of apparatuses in our time," Agamben sweepingly describes every element of contemporary capitalist society as belonging to one of two categories: living beings, and apparatuses in which the former are "incessantly captured." Agamben, 13. The philosopher sometimes seems to elide Foucault's definition of the term with the more colloquial understanding where an apparatus describes a singular device or object. For example, Agamben repeatedly refers to the cellular phone as an apparatus. Similarly, he notes that today, "the pen, writing, literature, philosophy, agriculture, cigarettes," and other objects and practices might be understood as apparatuses in their ability to "capture, orient, determine, in-

tercept, model, control, or secure the gestures, behaviors, opinions, or discourses of living beings." Agamben, 14. While Agamben's extension of Foucault is constructive in framing the contemporary relevance of the analyses contained in this book, the particular sense of the Foucaultian apparatus forwarded here diverges from Agamben's revisions. In the analyses that follow, singular objects or practices can never be an apparatus. Rather, the apparatus is always a structural or organizational ensemble that networks singular objects, practices and more into instrumentalized interrelation.

32   See Martin Jay, *Downcast Eyes: The Denigration of Vision in Twentieth-Century French Thought* (Los Angeles: University of California Press, 1994), 456–491, for a concise history of the emergence of apparatus theory in *Cahiers du Cinema*, as well as the influence of Althusserian Marxism and psychoanalysis therein.

33   Christian Metz, *The Imaginary Signifier* (Indianapolis: Indiana University Press, 1977), 7. According to Metz, the goal of the film industry is to create "good

term cinema an *imaginary* medium (in the psycho-analytic sense of the term) entailing the formation of desire for the ego-ideal in relation to an understanding of one's own image.[34] While the cinematic institution orients audience consciousness, the audience, as part of the institution, orients the character of the standard Hollywood film as a function of spectatorial desire.[35] In sum, the cinematic institution is meant to describe the iterative exchange between money and subjective affect through which averages are established and filmic aesthetics are naturalized. This exchange brackets spectatorial experience as a function of images beholden to audience desire and the financial well being of the film industry.

object relations" within its audience—to create image-objects that prompt positive cathexes from the viewing public. This fact becomes a shared ambition between the psychic composition of the audience and the financial composition of the film industry. This elided entity is what Metz terms the "cinematic institution." Metz writes, "Let me insist once again, the cinema institution is not just the cinema industry (which works to fill cinemas, not to empty them), it is also the mental machinery—another industry—which spectators 'accustomed to the cinema' have internalized historically and which has adapted them to the consumption of films." Metz, 7.

34   Metz wrote: "A technique of the imaginary, but in two senses. In the ordinary sense of the word, as a whole critical tendency culminating in the work of Edgar Morin has demonstrated, because most films consist of fictional narratives and because all films depend even for their signifier on the primary imaginary of photography and phonography. In the Lacanian sense, too, in which the imaginary, opposed to the symbolic but constantly imbricated with it, designates the basic lure of the ego, the definitive imprint of a stage before the Oedipus complex (which also continues after it), the durable mark of the mirror which alienates man in his own reflection and makes him the double of his double, the subterranean persistence of the exclusive relation to the mother, desire as a pure effect of lack and endless pursuit, the initial core of the conscious (primal repression)." Metz, 3–4. Metz's work concentrates on the latter, the Lacanian, sense of the imaginary, springing from Metz's interpretation of Lacan's mirror-stage analysis. The mirror-stage describes the event in an infant's life in which he or she first recognizes his or her reflection in a mirror and therefore understands self-as-other or self-as-image. The composed image returns to the infant a cohesive understanding of self that exceeds the comparatively

rudimentary developmental state of the child. Thus, the self-image is instrumental in the formation of the ego-ideal, or the ideal self. Elaborating on Lacan, Metz explains the way in which cinema signifies as an imaginary by describing a point in an infant's development when the mother stands next to a child in front of the mirror and the infant is forced to identify both the self and a secondary identification of the reflected image of the other (44). Metz writes: "This other other is its (the child's) guarantee that the first is really it: by her authority, her sanction, in the register of the symbolic, subsequently by the resemblance between her mirror image and the child's (both have a human form). Thus the child's ego is formed by identification with its like, and this in two senses simultaneously, metonymically and metaphorically: the other human being who is in the glass, the own reflection which is and is not the body, which is like it." (45) Building on this complex associative moment, wherein the infant's ego is formed by identifying with and through the self-as-image (metaphorically), and, *metonymically* through the other and the other-as-image, Metz theorizes that the cinematic imaginary is always enrolled in the desire for the ego-ideal, as cinema always presents to the spectator the other-as-image. Metz's corollary to the mirror-stage training is the beginning of a theoretical trajectory that helps him speculate on how the spectator has object relations with the imaginary objects of cinema, thus enabling subjective identification in relation to the conventions of the imaginary on the movie screen.

35   "It [cinema] also exists as our product, the product of the society which consumes it, as an orientation of consciousness, whose roots are unconscious, and without which we would be unable to understand the overall trajectory which founds the institution and accounts for its continuing existence." Metz, 93.

Both the Foucaultian apparatus and the sense of the term deriving from film theory have provided guidance here. Indeed, in a manner that I suspect would be acceptable by the forebearers of both theoretical trajectories, these two senses of the apparatus are liberally combined in the methodology of this book. Urban planning and economic policies are analyzed in relation to media aesthetics and economics, the subjectivities each set of interests implicate, and New York's material urban environment. None of these policies, economies, or environments is exhaustively analyzed. Rather, the points of their interrelation are highlighted. It may be impossible to describe the totality of an apparatus. The extents of the interests and forces that such an assemblage aggregates, usurps and puts into relation is perhaps too vast. More within the realm of possibility is to provide an analysis that tracks a series of iterative and discursive motions through an apparatus. Through repetition, the tracery of these trajectories might cumulatively achieve resolution. The latter is the objective here.

This book has been written in two parts. Part 1, *The Apparatus*, provides the core historical and theoretical crucible of the book. *The Apparatus* examines policies intended to draw on-location media productions to New York during John Lindsay's mayoral tenure, as well as a collection of representationally rich documents that were produced by Lindsay's planning commission and associated groups. My argument describes conceptual, aesthetic, and interpersonnel relationships between these two areas of policy, and between those policies, contemporaneous business mechanisms in media production, and larger prevalent cultural attitudes towards imagery and media at the time. Central to my argument is that running through these disparate areas of concern are latent assumptions about subjectivity—that of the media audience and that of the New Yorker. These subject positions are understood to be conduits through which flow the relationships my analysis vivifies. Among the primary documents analyzed in this first part of the book are the 1969 *Plan for New York City*, and a film-version of the *Plan* titled *What Is the City but the People?*

Part 2, *The City*, is composed of three essays, each tracing actors, spaces or ideas emerging from the crucible of activity described in the first part of this book, and each forwarding explicit architectural or urban analyses. In each chapter, I search for evidence of the apparatus described in Part 1 in New York's built environment, and in the subject positions implicated in the built environment. Read separately, each essay in Part 2 of this book assumes a theoretical lens that may seem difficult to resolve with those of the remaining two parts. My intention is to grant due diligence to my objects of study, allowing each to accumulate its own set of conceptual alliances, while demonstrating the capacity of the apparatus to usurp and make relational heterogeneity.

The first essay of Part 2 is titled *Spectatorship*. This essay chronicles a 1972 study of the effects of New York City's 1960 zoning policy that granted developers a floor-area-ratio bonus for providing plaza space at the ground level. Mayor Lindsay's Planning Commission asked William Whyte, an urbanist and sociologist who had previous worked with the Commission on the 1969 *Plan for New York City*, to conduct the study. The essay contends that Whyte's prior experience with Lindsay's Planning Commission was formative of his methodological approach. Isolating the plaza at Mies van der

Rohe's Seagram Building as an exemplar worthy
of study, Whyte's methods entailed the use of stationary and hand-held film cameras to monitor
the daily activities and occupations of the plaza.
Whyte then analyzed his film footage and made
suggestions for improvements to the Planning
Commission based on his filmic observations.
Spectatorship contextualizes Whyte's study within
his larger intellectual disposition, analyzes his description of the Seagram study, and provides a formal analysis of qualities he may have observed at
the Seagram Building. The chapter contends that
because Whyte privileged film as a medium for
observation, his design suggestions implicated
plaza spaces that provide a physical environment
from which the surrounding city can be figured
as a proto-cinematic experience—an experience
meeting the expectations of urban subjects first
exposed to New York through media enabled by
Mayor Lindsay's earlier policies. Whyte's suggestions were implemented in a 1975 revision to the
city's incentive zoning policy. Thus the spatial
qualities he isolated are common throughout New
York City.

The second essay is titled *Scenography*. The
essay discusses the appearance of historic and often blighted areas within New York in film and
television in the late 1960s and early 1970s—a development that would not have occurred to such
an extent without the conjuncture of Lindsay's
media production policies and specific business
developments in Hollywood discussed in Part 1
of this book. *Scenography* connects the media exposure granted historic or blighted locales to the
parallel development of an elevated cultural valuation of these areas evident in the establishment of
the 1965 New York City Landmarks Preservation

Commission, and later policies produced by groups within Mayor Lindsay's administration. During and shortly after Lindsay's tenure, the Office for Lower Manhattan Development, the Urban Design Group and the Office Midtown Planning and Development, all established by Lindsay, drafted "special district" zoning resolutions for areas such as Greenwich Street in lower Manhattan and Little Italy. An extension of the preservationist sentiment evident in the establishment of the Landmarks Preservation Commission, many of these special district zoning resolutions sought to channel development such that the scenographic appearance of the historic streetscape was preserved, precisely the aspect of the city being popularized in film and television at the time. Through an analysis of film, policy and media theory, *Scenography* argues that these developments created a city uniquely solicitous of the desire for urban lifestyle among New Yorkers first exposed to the city through media.

The final essay, *Ecology*, establishes a connection between the apparatus described in the first part of the book and emergent ecological thinking in Lindsay's Planning Commission. The essay begins with a discussion of a 1970 conference hosted by the Wenner-Gren Foundation in New York City titled "Restructuring the Ecology of a Great City." The conference was conceived by Jacqueline Robertson, then Chair of Mayor Lindsay's Office for Midtown Planning and Development, and the keynote was philosopher Gregory Bateson, one of the foremost voices in the ecological movement of the 1960s and 1970s. Critical among Bateson's contributions to ecological thought is his inclusion of the circulation of *cultural ideas*, or what he called "ecology of mind," in determining the health of the physical environment. *Ecology* contends that Bateson's thought complimented urban planning and design in New York City in complex and interrelated ways, weaving through and connecting the proto-ecology of real-estate economics, the urban ecology of interrelated programs in the city, and the "ecology of mind" of planners and the city's public. In regards to the later, the *ecology of mind*, the mediatic character of policies and urban environments encouraged by Lindsay's Planning Commission played a critical role in tuning societal sensibilities. This chapter includes an analysis of a special district zoning resolution for Manhattan's theatre district drafted by Jacqueline Robertson's Office of Midtown Planning and Development, and culminates with a discussion of an unrealized project from the late 1970s titled The City at 42nd Street. The project involved Lindsay Administration alumni, Jacqueline Robertson, Donald Elliot, and Richard Weinstein, and vivifies the Administration's ambition to cultivate the theatre district as a media ecology through which the city's urban ecology might be repaired. If the ubiquity of mediated representations of New York City constitutes a vast second-nature, this chapter asserts that such naturalization reflects the application of an ecological model from the natural sciences in urban planning and design.

Apparatus theories, like those of urban spectacle, are totalizing in their critique. For good reason, the apparatus theory of cinema is broadly assumed to be a dead end by contemporary media theorists.[36] It leaves no position of artistic or political agency throughout the production of main-

36   For one critique of the apparatus theory of cinema, see Richard Allen, *Projecting Illusion: Film Spectatorship and the Impression of Reality* (Cambridge: Cambridge University Press, 1995), 7–39. Allen's critique primarily targets the work of Jean-Louis Baudry, arguing that the theorist's seminal work in developing the apparatus theory of cinema is fraught with misappropriations of

stream media. Critic, artist, and audience alike are rendered blindly complicit in the circulation of corrosively ideological aesthetic confections. Similarly, spectacle, especially in today's ubiquitously mediated environment, is inescapable. Analysis of the ways in which contemporary urban visuality mystifies reality, underwriting interests of capital and power, are only too accessible for the critical theorist. Perhaps in an act of willful naiveté, this book borrows from these theoretical trajectories, while refusing to accept their conventionalized ends. Instead, this analysis is intended to articulate an expanded field of action, one in which the representations so often derided by theorists of urban spectacle may be reconceived as objects of design, and the apparatuses through which these representations flow might be exploited.[37]

Such willful naiveté recognizes my intended audience, including urban designers and architects—those responsible for the design of the city's built environment, and those whose contributions might be rendered ineffectual by mere critique. By analyzing one bracketed set of circumstances through which New York City and its mediated representation became intermeshed, this book asks designers to reconceptualize the agency and

ideas from Althusser and Lacan, and employs tautological reasoning that debases the fundamental integrity of the theorization. This book draws more heavily on Christian Metz's theory of the cinematic institution, borrowing from apparatus theory an understanding of the exchange between economics, cinematic aesthetics and subjective affect described therein. While critiques like those of Allen are sound, this book attempts to borrow from apparatus theory in a discerning and operative manner, excavating those aspects of the argument that are salient and sustained by the materials analyzed herein.

37   Such exploitation should be understood as a distinct strategy from that characterized by Giorgio Agamben as "the well-meaning discourse on technology, which asserts that the problem with apparatuses can be reduced to the question of their correct use." Agamben, 21. Agamben's as-

sertion is that an apparatus (or device) such as a cellular phone cannot simply be used correctly or incorrectly, as its ideological alliances derive largely from the modes of subjectification the device implicates. Thus, use of the device alone eviscerates any subjective agency that might be exercised in correct or incorrect use. In the sense of the term extended in this book, a singular device can never be an apparatus. Rather, following Foucault, devices, subjectivities, practices, legal proceedings, and more are enrolled in an apparatus, and the network of interconnections between these nodes is the apparatus itself. Thus, the trajectory advocated here should be read less as a well-meaning solicitation of "correct use," and more as a call for activity that will manipulate apparatuses on a structural level—producing new subjectivities, practices, legal frameworks and more.

alliances of the representations they produce as cultural products that can be complexly intertwined with urban reality. To be sure, the field of relationships between New York and its mediated representation described in this book is now a matter of history. Provided here is a still image—a frozen frame*work* of relationships that are fleeting and dynamic. Today's designers enter a reconstituted field of relationships, and one composed of urbanisms and media ecologies that are even more complex. This book provides a methodological exemplar through which contemporary relationships between mediated representations and material urban reality might be understood, wielded or designed. Today, more than ever, many of the capacities that have historically been granted the architecture of the city—to frame common experience, to represent its public—is now shared by mediated representations. Rather than deny, lament or resist this disciplinary slippage, this book urges architects and urban designers to engage the vaporized disciplinary border between urban reality and representation as the context in which any project for the contemporary city must be conceived.

Part 1

The Apparatus

The Apparatus

"If you want to know why I am so happy doing this picture in New York," offered Norman Lear, producer of the 1968 film *The Night They Raided Minsky's*, "ask the Mayor."[1] The primary location for Lear's film was in Manhattan at East 26th Street between 1st and 2nd Avenues. After beginning production, Lear and his company learned that their film location was slated for demolition while the movie was still being shot, part of a continuing wave of urban renewal that had indelibly altered New York throughout the preceding two decades.[2] The policy's transformation of the city seemed unstoppable, much to the dismay of the *Minsky's* production team. But this particular instance of urban renewal was delayed by an unusual development. New York's mayor, John Lindsay, came to the rescue of *The Night They Raided Minsky's*—halting the urban renewal project and allowing Lear's company to finish shooting their film. Thus, as bulldozers leveled the south side of the street, the north side was turned over to Lear's art directors to create what one journalist called *Minsky-land*—a recreation of what the neighborhood might have looked like in 1925.[3] Evincing a nostalgic sentiment for a bygone Gotham of tenements and continental immigrants, the block soon became a popular tourist destination. John Lindsay soon earned a reputation as a mayor who was not afraid to engage two areas of policy more vigorously than any previous New York mayor: the physical design of the city and the policy governing film and television productions set in New York (figs. 1-2).

The Lindsay administration governed New York City from 1966 to 1973. Famously, this period coincided with the national "urban crisis," an era of physical, economic and social decline in cities nation-wide. Thus, Lindsay's tenure is often remembered for the breadth of crises that it witnessed—from the transit strike of 1966 to the Hard Hat Riots of 1970, all set against a backdrop of mounting racial tension, fiscal insolvency, and urban blight.[4] But Lindsay's tenure was also one of marked optimism. His liberal Republican

1   "The Advantages of Making Films in New York," *New York Magazine*, December 1967, 35–36.

2   Urban renewal began as a federal policy enacted by Congress in 1949 in order to channel capital development funds to the nation's struggling cities during their postwar decline. In New York, urban renewal was managed through the City Planning Commission, an agency under the direct oversight of the office of the mayor. Urban renewal projects typically entailed the wholesale leveling of decrepit neighborhoods, replacing them with subsidized housing or late-modernist development. Between 1949 and 1959 alone, the city spent more than 141 million in federal dollars on urban renewal projects and more than one billion in private investor dollars. See Bill Rose, "The Fifties," in *Planning the Future of New York City: A Conference Celebrating the 40th Anniversary of the New York City Planning Commission* (New York, 1979), 24–28.

3   "The Advantages of Making Films in New York," 35–36.

4   See Sam Roberts, "City in Crisis I," in *America's Mayor: John V. Lindsay and the Reinvention of New York*, ed. Sam Roberts (New York: Columbia University Press, 2010), 10–25 for a review of the state of New York during the urban crisis when John Lindsay took office, and see Steven Weisman, "City in Crisis II," in *America's Mayor: John V. Lindsay and the Reinvention of New York*, ed. Sam Roberts (New York: Columbia University Press, 2010), 192–213 for a review of the crises during Lindsay's tenure.

William Friedkin. *The Night They Raided Minsky's*, 1968. Frame enlargement.

fig.
1

William Friedkin. *The Night They Raided Minsky's*, 1968. Frame enlargement.

fig.
2

administration drew young and talented individuals to public service like that of no previous mayor. With this influx of talent came
new and innovative thoughts on urban policy.

It was within this context that the city created policies intended to alleviate the bureaucracy and corruption that had made location-shot film and television production in New York financially prohibitive throughout the previous twenty years. Lindsay and his staff
made unprecedented concessions to the media industry to provide
a comfortable and profitable business environment. Also during
Lindsay's tenure, the city drafted a wealth of innovative planning
and urban design documents. The administration's heightened interest in urban design attracted some of the city's most renowned
architects to public service and won the admiration of architecture

critics.[5] While the collection of planning documents produced under Lindsay is vast and diverse, one aspect common to many is a tendency to understand the public's engagement with the city in various
ways that reflect aesthetic and intellectual influences of visual media. Perhaps unconsciously, the architects, urbanists, and bureau-
crats Lindsay drew to service from various backgrounds drafted urban design and planning policies that conceptualized the city, and
its public, through various mediatic registers. Hence, Lindsay's planning policy has a complexly intertwined relationship to the administration's policy regarding media production in New York. Amplifying the significance of this blend of media production and planning
policy was a developing financial and interpersonnel symbiosis between the city and the film and television industry. During the Lindsay administration New York was inviting media production to its
streets, while conceiving of the public's engagement of those streets
through various mediatic registers, and yoking the financial interests of the city to those of the film and television industry.

The conjuncture of policies and financial alliances under Lindsay provides a telling lens through which to reexamine the relationship between the material New York and its mediated representation.
The years since Lindsay's tenure have proven his media production
and urban planning policies effective on several registers: economic, juridical, and aesthetic. The contention here is that these effects
must be understood as they engage one another *discursively*—as a
fluid and iterative exchange between the financial stability of New
York and the media industry, the methods of conceptualizing urbanism evident in the policies of Lindsay's Planning Commission, and
the subjective affect of the media spectator and the urban subject.
The engagement *between* these disparate interests and effects constitutes the apparatus of interest here. Through the explication of such
an apparatus, a complex relationship between New York, its mediated representation, and the urban public can be described. Rooted
in interrelated historic developments, this relationship between New
York and its mediated self was profoundly formative of the city as it
stands today.

Executive Order Number 10

Upon his inauguration, Mayor Lindsay inherited a declining
city. New York was plagued with corruption, poor race relations,
poverty, crumbling infrastructure, and impending environmental
crisis.[6] Confounding any attempt by the mayor's administration to
deal with the city's growing list of woes was a mounting budgetary

5   See Ada Louise Huxtable, "Adding Up the Score,"   6   John V. Lindsay, Speech at the Urban American
     The New York Times, January 20, 1974.   Conference in Washington, D.C., September 12,
                                                                1966, in Folder 153, Box 63, John V. Lindsay Pa-
                                                                pers, Yale University Manuscripts and Archives.

dilemma. More than a decade of middle-class white flight to the sub-urbs and a dwindling manufacturing sector had taken its toll on the city's tax base.[7] And at the state level a policy of funds dispersion that favored rural and suburban areas ensured that New York City consistently sent more money to Albany than it received.[8]

Nowhere was the bleak outlook more pronounced than in the urban environment. The City Planning Commission's 1969 *Plan for New York City* begins

It is obvious enough that there is a great deal wrong. The air is polluted. The streets are dirty and choked with traffic. The subways are jammed. The waters of the rivers and bays are fouled. There is a severe shortage of housing. The municipal plant is long past its prime.[9]

The problems with the built environment were abundantly clear to the commission. Less clear was how to acquire the funds needed to rectify those problems. A November 1, 1968, memo from John Lindsay explained that the planning commission would be provided a record allowance of 400 million dollars for capital improvements in 1969. This sum amounted to only one-quarter of the 1.6 billion dollars the commission required.[10] By 1969 the planning commission estimated that in order to meet the capital improvement, housing, and infrastructural needs of New York over the next decade, they would need 52 billion dollars in funding above what could be provided by the city.[11] Without further recourse, the commission looked toward the federal urban renewal and Model Cities programs for relief.[12]

Meanwhile, the office of the mayor was left to find ways of promoting new economic activity in the city that could be taxed to fund the city's struggling offices. In 1966, within this economic climate, Mayor Lindsay signed Executive Order Number 10, a measure intent on drawing the film and television industry to New York through the creation of the New York City Mayor's Office of Film, Theatre, and Broadcasting. While the years since Lindsay signed Executive Order Number 10 have witnessed several campaigns and tax incentive programs to draw the film and television industry to American cities, Lindsay's actions were both innovative and unique at the time.

7   Donald H. Elliott, *Critical Issues*, vol. 1 of *The Plan for the City of New York* (New York: New York City Planning Commission, 1971), 4.
8   Lindsay, Speech, September 12, 1966.
9   Elliott, *Critical Issues*, 4.
10   Memorandum, by John Lindsay to the City Planning Commission, November 1, 1968, in Roll A-6, John Lindsay Microfilm, New York City Municipal Archive.
11   Elliott, *Critical Issues*, 23.

12   Carter Horsley, "The Sixties," in *Planning the Future of New York City*, 29–36. The Model Cities program was created in 1966 as part of President Johnson's war on poverty. The program was administered by the federal Department of Housing and Urban Development (HUD) and was meant to improve and fund the coordination of existing federally funded urban programs, such as Urban Renewal, with locally produced planning. The program advocated the participation of local citizens in the planning process and extended beyond the physical aspects of the city to fund the delivery of social services.

The American film industry was born in New York in the late nineteenth century. But by 1932 the rise of the Hollywood studios largely spelled the end of location film production in New York.[13] The reasons were both technical and political: the sound, depth-of-field, and film-speed technologies that were required to make city shooting advantageous had yet to be developed; and New York was a notoriously corrupt location for film production.[14] Throughout the decades after 1932, solutions were developed to alleviate the technical detriments to shooting in the city.[15] Mayor Lindsay sought to alleviate the political detriments with Executive Order 10.

Prior to Lindsay's executive order, filming in New York required as many as fifty different permits, and productions could face daily fines and police shakedowns of as much as 400 dollars a day.[16] Meanwhile, union corruption made labor in the cinema arts in New York cost prohibitive as compared to Los Angeles.[17] Lindsay's policy condensed film-production permitting to one standard document that would apply to all filming locations.[18] The mayor revoked media censorship powers from municipal agencies, negotiated with the local industry labor unions to offer competitive rates, and even created a division in the police department composed of officers specially trained in the "cinema arts." This special task force was trained to "reroute traffic, keep back onlookers, or persuade pedestrians to behave like believable New Yorkers in a street scene."[19] Meanwhile, the mayor began a letter-writing campaign to media industry executives, personally inviting them to film their productions in New York.[20] The extent to which Lindsay's administration streamlined the economic and bureaucratic conditions for media production in New York was unprecedented.

To the keen observer, Lindsay's actions may have been anticipated. During his campaign, Lindsay endorsed an effort to build new post-production facilities for film and television in New York City.

13   James Sanders, *Celluloid Skyline: New York and the Movies* (New York: Alfred A. Knopf, 2003), 343. Exceptions did occur, most notably Jules Dassin's 1948 film noir *The Naked City*. With much fanfare, and nearly twenty years after the studios relocated to Hollywood, the film brought mass location shooting to Manhattan. At the time, the film was widely understood to be remarkable in its insistence on location shooting. After the film studios moved to Hollywood, productions that were *fictionally* set in New York were usually shot on backlot recreations of the city that had been built at great expense and detail by major studios such as Paramount and 20th Century Fox. Films from this period include classics such as RKO's *Swing Time* (1936, with Fred Astaire and Ginger Rogers) and King Vidor's *The Fountainhead* (1949). Narratives set within New York remained common and quite popular. The popularity of these films made the possibility of returning to location shooting in New York all the more attractive when the opportunity

arose. See Sanders, 44–84, for a description of the major studio's efforts in recreating New York in the art departments and backlots of Hollywood.

14   From the advent of the sound film in the 1920s until the development of the directional microphone, noise pollution was the most immediate detriment to shooting in the city. In California, where construction space was abundant, sealed soundstages became a more appropriate shooting location. See Sanders, 44–45.

15   Sanders, 341.

16   "New York—The Big Set," *Newsweek*, May 29, 1967, 86–87.

17   "Movie Men Like Our Town: 'It's Alive,'" *World Journal Tribune*, April 23, 1967.

18   Remarks by Mayor John V. Lindsay at the opening luncheon for the 1966 convention of the National Association of Theatre Owners, September 28, 1966. Folder 167, Box 63, John V. Lindsay Papers, Yale University Manuscripts and Archives.

19   "Movie Men Like Our Town."

By 1967 plans were underway for these facilities. An enormous complex called Cinema Center was slated for construction on the site of the old Madison Square Garden. The design by architect Charles Luckman was to occupy a full west-Midtown block, with two thirty-nine-story office towers bracketing the complex on the east and west sides and a seven-story structure that would span the middle of the block and house film studios, two live-action theatres, and four motion picture theatres.[21] Although Cinema Center was never built, its presence among Lindsay's campaign promises helps to clarify the depth of the mayor's ambitions to draw film and television productions to the city. And recurrent news of plans for the complex garnered a substantial amount of public attention, adding visibility to the mayor's larger efforts to attract media production (fig. 3).

Indeed, visibility was a primary tactic in the mayor's efforts. Lindsay was notoriously charismatic, with an obvious flair for the camera. One *Newsweek* article described Lindsay as "movie-star-handsome."[22] Another reported that he attended industry events such as the Hollywood Radio and Television Society luncheon at the Beverly Hills Hotel, where he wooed production company executives.[23] At a 1969 Motion Picture Association of American (MPAA)

fig. 3

Irving Michael Felt (left) and architect Charles Luckman (right) with a presentation drawing of Cinema Center. *The New York Times*, March 8, 1966.

20 Remarks by Mayor John V. Lindsay at the opening luncheon for the 1966 convention of the National Association of Theatre Owners, September 28, 1966.

21 "Cinema City Planned for Old Garden Site," *The New York Times*, March 8, 1966. Cinema Center was funded by Irving Michael Felt, president of the Madison Square Garden Corporation and brother of former City Planning Commission chairman James Felt.

22 "New York—The Big Set," 86–87.

23 "Mayor Lindsay Charms H'wood, But Did He Sell 'Em N.Y. as Location?" *Variety Magazine,* November 22, 1967.

celebration of the seventy-fifth anniversary of commercial films, the mayor was even awarded an achievement medal by MPAA president Jack Valenti.[24] Lindsay's movie-star fraternizing aligns with other events, such as his headline-garnering action on the *Minsky's* site and reports that he shared his office with director George Seaton as the latter filmed *Up the Down Staircase* (1967). Such lust for the limelight contributed to the popular conclusion that this was a mayor more suave than smart—one that, perhaps, just wanted to be in pictures.[25]

However, Lindsay's showmanship should not obscure the tact of his actions. The financial benefits of Lindsay's efforts were quickly realized. In the final months of 1966, film production levels in New York rose to an all-time high, adding 20 million dollars to the city economy.[26] In 1965 only eleven films were shot in New York, with only two of these reaching postproduction in local studios. In 1967, 223 permits were issued for feature films and 633 for television and commercial productions.[27] Although the long-term economic effects of these policies are difficult to calculate, when one considers that the motion picture and television economy in New York had reached a level of 500 million dollars a year by 1980, the contribution of Lindsay's policies seems significant.[28] By one account, film productions led by director Sidney Lumet alone had given back to the city an estimated 200 million dollars in direct tax revenue by 1984.[29]

This economic success was not merely serendipitous. Lindsay's policy complemented larger shifts within the business apparatus of Hollywood. This was particularly true of trends in Hollywood film production. Throughout the 1960s, with the growing ubiquity of television in the American home, the film industry experienced a marked decrease in ticket sales. Hollywood's financial troubles piqued in 1962, when movie attendance hit a nation-wide low.[30] Increasingly, the viewing public met the historical epics that were the hallmark product of the Hollywood studios with less and less enthusiasm. Thus, the film industry sought to explore new genres. The Hollywood studios

24   Briefing to Mayor Lindsay on the proceedings of the MPAA's celebration of the 75th anniversary of the motion picture. April 10, 1969. Folder 854, Box 83, John V. Lindsay Papers, Yale University Manuscripts and Archives.

25   Lindsay, in fact, went on to play the role of Senator Donnovan in Otto Preminger's 1975 film *Rosebud.* Preminger's previous film, *Such Good Friends* (1971), was filmed in New York under the stewardship of Executive Order 10.

26   "For the Movie-Makers," *World Journal Tribune,* April 23, 1967.

27   "Watch Out–," *American Way* 1, no. 3. 7–9.

28   "Koch Predicts Astoria Studio Rebirth," *The New York Times,* September 6, 1980, 12. The economic boon for New York from Lindsay's policies was not limited to direct tax revenues on film productions. A 1968 article on the mayor's work to bring film to the city appeared in *American Way,* the American

Airlines Magazine, directly indicating the cross-pollination of Lindsay's policy and tourism within the city. The article points to the recent shooting of *Up the Down Staircase* as an enticement for travelers to spend their next vacation, and their money, in New York: "It was a ball for the fortunate tourists and natives who happened in on the beautiful Miss Dennis while she was at work. And there will be many more such happenings in and around the landmarks of New York." "Watch Out–". 8.

29   "Sidney Lumet: Film Prince of the City," *The New York Times,* June 7, 1984, 17. This estimate was Lumet's own. Most films comprising this figure were produced after Executive Order 10, but Lumet's figure includes tax revenues from films dating back to 1956.

30   David Parkinson, *History of Film* (New York: Thames and Hudson, 1996), 221. Industry ticket sales were 900 million dollars in 1962.

began acting primarily as distribution centers for independent movies that were produced around the nation. By 1967, these independent-
ly produced films accounted for 51.1 percent of all feature releases by
the major studios.[31] This shift by the industry was coupled in 1967
with the Motion Picture Association of America's repeal of the Production Code (also called the Hays Code)—a set of standards that
had been implemented in the 1930s to ensure "decency" in motion
pictures. The production code censored violence, drug use, and nu-
dity in films and actively discouraged moral ambiguity in filmic narratives.

Mayor Lindsay's executive order worked in accord with these
larger shifts in the film industry. Studio decentralization encouraged
filmmaking in New York, and the films enabled by the mayor's policies later helped to turn the fortunes of the struggling film industry.
At a time when spectators were becoming less receptive to the standard Hollywood production, Mayor Lindsay's policies enabled filmmakers like Martin Scorsese, Francis Ford Coppola, and Woody Allen to produce tremendously successful location-shot films in New
York City. Largely associated with the New Hollywood movement
in cinema, these directors created New York movies that earned the
studios millions and aided in Hollywood's economic recovery.[32]

Meanwhile, the end of the Production Code made the *content*
of many films shot in the city after Executive Order 10 possible. Dystopic urban films such as John Schlesinger's *Midnight Cowboy* (1969),
William Friedkin's *The French Connection* (1971), and Martin Scorsese's *Taxi Driver* (1976) were soon prevalent at the movie theatre.
These films portrayed issues contextual to New York at the time—
such as crime, prostitution, and urban decadence—that simply
could not have been depicted under the Hays Code. New Hollywood directors brought to their treatment of these issues various
filmic techniques from American underground film, the French
New Wave and other avant-garde influences that emerged outside
of the mainstream Hollywood production system. These techniques, from disjunctive montage sequencing, to complex visual
distortions, to manipulations of cinema's conventional temporality, proved uniquely effective in representing New York's turbulent
physical and social reality cinematically. Revealing the contextual
blight of New York on the silver screen proved profitable for the film
industry, which encouraged studios to continue funding productions shot in New York, thus fueling the city's economy. In effect,
the city turned its dystopic conditions, which largely arose from
a lack of finances, into a revenue-generating opportunity. Thus
the city and the Hollywood production system—both in a state of

31   David E. James, *Allegories of Cinema: American*   32   James, 26–27.
     Film in the Sixties (Princeton: Princeton Universi-
     ty Press, 1989), 26.

crisis—found within their mutual precarity an opportunity to be mutually ameliorative.[33]

Even more profound than the economic impact of films produced in New York at this time was their effect on cinema audiences. These films contributed to a revolutionizing of the type of production spectators around the country became accustomed to viewing. Gritty and "realistic" location-shot New York City films such as *Midnight Cowboy* stood in stark contrast to the historically based epics that were the fading staple of the Hollywood production system as late as 1963.[34] The pageantry and stagey aesthetic of the latter could not be more divergent from the nearly documentary or complexly edited character of films shot in New York in the late 1960s and early 1970s. Equally, these New York City films contrasted those previous that were either actually or fictionally set in the city. The contextual grit and vice of films such as *Taxi Driver* significantly revise the portrait of an enchanted city found in the backlot-shot New York City musicals of the previous few decades (e.g., *Singin' in the Rain*), or in the shadowy New York of the film noir cycle. Thus, taken together, the films resultant from Lindsay's executive order constituted a new *image* of New York in popular media—an image that deeply leveraged the city's contextual conditions. This new mediated image would eventually alter the sort of urban narrative that cinema spectators associated with the city, coloring popular expectation of the material New York among media audiences.

Such a modification of New York's popular image may have been one of Mayor Lindsay's motivations behind Executive Order 10. In his 1969 book about his mayoral experience, *The City*, Lindsay wrote that American cities suffered from a lack of positive narratives about urbanism within cultural discourse. Lindsay cites novels such as *Moll Flanders* as indicative of the prevailing pejorative attitude with which Anglo-American narratives have treated the city.[35] In nuanced reasoning befitting a media-savvy politician, the mayor argued that the derogatory popular image of cities in American culture, and their associated stigma of moral decadence, essentially resulted in an electorate supportive of representation that favored suburban and rural constituencies. This, in turn, resulted in anti-urban policy and—*critically*—policy that under-funded urban

1

Part

33 David James has theorized that such conditions, when both the dominant mode of cinematic production and society at large are in states of crisis, can give rise to an allegorical relationship between the two. James wrote: "Films made in periods such as this (in times of crisis) frequently attempt to negotiate with surrounding social and cinematic changes, and even when they are not explicitly about the search for a satisfactory mode of production, their plots often have some metaphorical relation to their own manufacture. Consequently, as the site of conflict or arbitration between alternative productive possibilities, they invite an allegorical reading in which a given filmic trope—a camera style or an editing pattern—is understood as the trace of a social practice." James, 14.

34 This was the year that Joseph Mankiewicz's *Cleopatra* debuted. The film was a major financial disappointment for 20th Century Fox.

35 John V. Lindsay, *The City* (New York: Norton, 1970), 50–60. This was not an isolated argument for Lindsay. He repeated it on several occasions, including at a 1966 speech at the Urban American Conference in Washington, DC. See Lindsay, Speech, September 12, 1966.

areas while monetarily incentivizing the suburbs. As examples, Lindsay cited policies such as the massive federal funding of the interstate highway system, which enabled population dispersal, and the postwar FHA grant subsidies of low-interest loans for suburban homes.

Lindsay went so far as to suggest that the repeated derogatory narratives of urbanism within American culture affected American psychology. Lindsay wrote: ". . . it is historically true: in the American psychology, the city has been a basically suspect institution, reeking of the corruption of Europe, totally lacking that sense of spaciousness and innocence of the frontier and the rural landscape."[36] The agility with which Lindsay's reasoning traverses and interconnects psychological, political and economic registers is revealing. Apparently, for Lindsay issues of urban policy and finance were intricately intertwined with the psychic resonance of cities among Americans. The psychology of Americans, their subsequent voting habits, and the economic policies that resulted were richly interrelated within an underlying apparatus. With this in mind, the mayor seems unlikely to have been oblivious to the psychic associations attached to his own city that would be affected by the media productions enabled by Executive Order 10. Indeed, the mayor's thoughts suggest that he may have viewed the manipulation of the city's image in media as an indirect vehicle for change in the material New York, as the new media productions would change audience attitudes, their voting habits, and subsequent urban policy.

Thus, at first glance the motivations behind Executive Order 10 may seem clear—a nearly desperate attempt to draw taxable activity to New York in an era of blight and economic decline. However, with a review of the interests and concerns surrounding Lindsay's policy, the effects of his action are revealed to be discursive: complex, multifaceted, and interrelated. Lindsay's Executive Order intertwined the financial interests of New York to those of the Hollywood studios and affected the way New York was portrayed in popular culture, thus inflecting the city's psychic resonance among Americans. The latter outcome also benefited from the alliance with another, rather unlikely, division of the city's government: the City Planning Commission. The planning commission was among the most financially needy of the government agencies under Lindsay that stood to benefit from media-related revenues, and the ideology behind their use of the funds they were granted is significant. By conceiving of New York through various mediatic registers in their planning policy, the commission played upon the expectations of those exposed to the city through film and television, and implanted mediatic understandings of the city within the material New York to be experienced by the urban subject. The apparatus emerged.

36   Lindsay, *The City*, 50.

The Threatened City

When Mayor Lindsay entered office in 1966, he did so within a political climate that was increasingly characterized by citizen activism around civil rights and the war in Vietnam.[37] This culture of protest extended into matters of city planning. The decades prior witnessed the heavy hand of Robert Moses in shaping New York's built environment. As the head of a series of administrative authorities, Moses stewarded vast urban renewal in the image of European modernist planning, as well as massive amounts of construction for automotive infrastructure. The aggressively top-down approach with which Moses extended his authority soon met the reproach of a newly activist urban public, culminating with Moses's famed confrontation with Jane Jacobs over the planned construction of the Lower Manhattan Expressway.[38] Noting the new context of citizen activism in matters of the built environment at the beginning of Lindsay's tenure, one architecture critic noted, "No more could the man on a specific street in a real neighborhood be easily ignored (in matters of city planning), as the power of the picket sign often captured as much airtime in the media as a Presidential news conference. It was where the action was."[39] The significance of the critic's statement is twofold. Individual members of the public could assume heightened influence in issues of the urban environment, and through media public activism could be made visible and effect popular opinion.

The planning policies of the Lindsay administration reflect a keen understanding of the elevated role media was assuming. In 1969, Lindsay's planning commission, under chairman Donald H. Elliott, released the *Plan for New York City*, the city's first master plan in the commission's thirty-one-year history. On August 22, 1967, more than a year before the new master plan was to be released, Lindsay penned letters to several prominent New York executives and philanthropists in solicitation of funding to make a documentary film based on the unfinished *Plan*. In one letter, the mayor explained, "Mr. Elliott and I firmly believe in the importance of gaining the greatest possible public understanding of the Plan. We have been persuaded that a documentary film will be the best possible method to educate the people of New York."[40] The latent implications of the mayor's solicitation are manifold. First, Lindsay made clear that the intention of the film was to educate New Yorkers. Hence, media was understood as a means of inflecting the behavior of the public. Further, Lindsay solicited funding for his film *before* the master plan on which it was to be based was finished. Before the plan was finalized, before the character of the city it framed was established, it was assumed that

Part

37   Horsley, 31.
38   See Jane Jacobs, *The Death and Life of Great American Cities* (New York: Random House, 1992).
39   Horsley, 32.

40   John V. Lindsay to Dr. E. Land, President of the Polaroid Company, August 22, 1967, in Roll A-7, John Lindsay Microfilm, New York City Municipal Archive.

the plan could be best communicated to the public through media, in this case film. Hence, the policies within the plan, and the city that these policies projected, were assumed to be inherently cinematic. The filmic medium and its relation to its audience were used as a conceptual paradigm to abstract the relationship between the city and the urban public. That relationship was now assumed to be mediatic, the individual on the street being the urban analog of the cinema spectator.

Such an awareness of the value of media as a model for conceptualizing the public's engagement with urbanism helps to explain the list of possible benefactors to whom Lindsay sent letters soliciting funding for his film. In addition to philanthropists and socialites, the list included the presidents of Polaroid (Dr. E. Land), Eastman Kodak (Louis Eilers), and the CEO of the CBS television network, William S. Paley.[41] The involvement of these individuals in matters of city planning may have been desirable because of their professional expertise. Each executive hailed from a company involved in some way in the production mediated imagery. For the same reason, each of these figures may have felt financially motivated to fund the mayor's film. Within the welcoming environment for the media arts that Lindsay had recently created, these executives had every reason to believe that New York was a ripening business environment and that Lindsay and his administration could be valuable allies.

This was particularly the case for William S. Paley. As early as 1967, *The New York Times* reported that CBS had plans to begin shooting major motion pictures in New York—a new venture that was undoubtedly influenced by Executive Order 10.[42] Paley's film company, which began production in 1968, was named *Cinema Center Films*— apparently borrowing the name of the proposed film facility in which CBS assumed its New York–centered production would be based. While no specific evidence links the mayor's funding solicitation to CBS business plans, one is tempted to recognize "back-room politics." By funding the mayor's documentary, Paley may have shown his gratitude to an administration that had enabled a new business venture for CBS, and ensured that Lindsay would remain an ally in the future.

But Paley's involvement in urban planning in New York was more complex than a simple financial alliance, predating the mayor's funding solicitation. In 1966, the year Executive Order 10 was signed, Lindsay established the Mayor's Taskforce on Urban Design. The taskforce was commissioned to produce a report on New York urban aesthetics that would be more far-reaching and proactive in its

41   Letters from John V. Lindsay to Joan Davidson (August 22, 1967), Dr. E. Land (August 29, 1967), Louis Eilers (August 29, 1967) and William S. Paley (August 22, 1967). Roll A–7, John Lindsay Microfilm, New York City Municipal Archive.

42   "Now Is Our Great Opportunity!" *The New York Times*, n.d. Newspaper clipping in Roll A–7, John Lindsay Microfilm, New York City Municipal Archive.

design considerations than a document produced by the planning
commission, whose primary purpose was zoning and development
policy. The taskforce—which included figures such as architects
Philip Johnson, I.M. Pei, Robert A.M. Stern, Jaquelin Robertson,
and *Architecture Forum* editor Walter McQuade—was chaired by
William S. Paley.[43]

Paley's appointment to chair an urban design taskforce is
curious. Indeed, the executive was known for his stewardship of
design at CBS.[44] And at the time of his appointment, Paley Park—
a vest-pocket park on 53rd Street designed by Robert Zion—was
planned for a 1967 opening. [45] The park was funded by Paley, and is
well known as a paradigmatic example of privately funded public
space in New York. Further, Paley was known as a prominent citizen of New York, and had previously served on various city commit-
tees. But these qualifications alone seem insufficient to place Paley
at the chair of a committee studying the city's built environment, one
staffed by prominent architects and urban designers. Critical to this
argument is that Paley's appointment to head the taskforce articulates an important conjuncture between the Lindsay Administration's media production policy and urban design policy. The success
of Paley's newly formed film company was in the best financial interest of both CBS and the city, and the media sensibility that Paley
brought to the Taskforce on Urban Design complimented the prevailing ideology with which the planning commission was conceptualizing the public's engagement with the city.

This latter point is consistent with the treatment of the city
within the publication produced by the Paley-led Taskforce on Urban Design, *The Threatened City: A Report on the Design of the City of
New York*.[46] The report is structured in four parts. The first section,
"The Troubles," diagnoses the problems with the urban environment;
the second section, "Opportunities," attempts to highlight areas rife
for change; the third section, "Towards a Method," begins to expli-
cate a new juridical structure for city planning; and the final section,
"Proposals," suggests policy changes. Walter McQuade chiefly tran-
scribed the report. But a television man's sensibility is evident from
the outset.

In the introduction to the report, the taskforce conveys the now
familiar portrayal of New York as the culture setter for the country:
Nowhere else are shaped so many of the things which
Americans buy, identify with, come to characterize

Part 1

---

43   Other members of the taskforce were James M.
     Clark, a noted New York businessman; Joan K.
     Davidson, trustee and president of the Kaplan
     Fund; Eli Jacobs, a lawyer and bureaucrat; George
     Lindsay, a lawyer and the mayor's brother; and
     Mrs. Albert A. List, wife of the founder of the Al-
     bert A. List foundation.

44   Dennis P. Doordon, "Design at CBS," *Design
     Issues* 6, no. 2: Spring, 1990, 4–17.
45   Maurice Carroll, "Paley Park: A Corner of Quiet
     Delights amid City's Bustle," *The New York Times*,
     September 20, 1967.
46   William S. Paley et al., *The Threatened City: A Re-
     port on the Design of the City of New York* (New
     York: 1967).

themselves by, ranging from the shape of one's hat to the songs teenagers wail. New York emits; the nation receives. A large example is the fact that a dozen American cities are even today planning or building groups of offices which they identify as "Rockefeller Centers," thirty years later.[47]

The description privileges the role of New York as an urban impression that is broadcast, as if through film or television, to the rest of the country—shaping consumerism and the way in which Americans understand themselves and their cultural identity. In the taskforce's statement, the city itself becomes a kind of mediated message. Significant among the New York City exports highlighted in the report is Rockefeller Center. The citation of the New York icon suggests that American's expectations of urbanism, and their expectations of urban subjectivity, may be prefigured through the mediated export of New York's urban image.

Such an understanding of the city is pervasive throughout *The Threatened City* in the form of a recurrent interest in grooming an image of the city that could be captured by visual media. Near the beginning of the report, its authors state plainly, "The committee's study ... was directed towards offenses to the eye,"[48] before continuing to describe various methods of approach to Manhattan (by airplane, train, car, and ocean liner) in proto-cinematic terms of urban promenade. The authors applaud the scenographic experience of the skyline view when circling the city by these various methods and indicate that the visual clarity of the skyline—its cohesiveness as a single iconic image that is immediately apprehended—allows one to understand him/herself in relation to the city through a dialogue of urban image and urban viewer. The problem with the interior city, according to the report, is that it fails to maintain this scenographic clarity, thus unsettling the urban subject who finds him/herself upon its streets.[49] To resolve this lack of visual clarity, the taskforce suggests greater legibility in urban iconography through standardization of signage and streetscape and calls for the development of scenic vistas at the corners of Central Park. Elsewhere, *The Threatened City* forwards further scopophilic suggestions: scenic vistas at Lincoln Center; controlled views of the city from the arterial highways; and the uniform painting of all city vehicles, kiosks, and telephone booths.

In order to ensure that the content of its report was implemented as policy, the taskforce suggested two major changes to the juridical structure of planning in New York City. First, the taskforce called for the creation of the Urban Design Council, a group of

47	Paley et al., 4.				49	Paley et al., 10.
48	Paley et al., 9.

aesthetic-minded citizens who could advise the mayor on issues of urban design. This council was established with William S. Paley as its first chairman and with I.M. Pei and Philip Johnson as members. The second major suggestion was for the establishment of the Urban Design Group, a cadre of elite professionals whose purpose was to take a proactive stance toward urban design in the city.[50] While the planning commission typically limited its intervention with the built environment to abstract zoning, the Urban Design Group could more directly ensure that the visual issues privileged in *The Threatened City* were implemented by proposing substantive revisions or counter-suggestions to privately planned development in the city. Again, the mayor accepted this suggestion, and the Urban Design Group was created with founding members Jaquelin Robertson, Jonathan Barnett, Richard Weinstein, and Myles Weintraub. Robertson was later named the first chair of the group.[51]

Throughout *The Threatened City*, the taskforce assumed a moralizing tone in its insistence on the visual, at one point urging that the work of the taskforce "not be shrugged off as cosmetic" but understood as "a meaningful way to make a proclamation, a show of determination that the city is taking its visual destiny in hand."[52] One might ask: a proclamation to whom? Read in context with the taskforce's introductory statement—"New York emits, the nation receives."[53]—the insistence on the cosmetic might be understood as a moral mandate for the grooming of an urban imaginary to be disseminated to New Yorkers and the rest of the country through visual media.

Such a moralizing tone when discussing urban aesthetics—at a time when the city was rife with so many social, economic, and ecological issues—smacks of the latent influence of Kevin Lynch's 1960 book *The Image of the City*. In Lynch's book, visual recognition of the urban environment is codified to give "its possessor an important sense of emotional security."[54] Lynch notes that a clear environmental image can give the urban subject "an harmonious relationship between himself and the outside world."[55] In *The Threatened City*, Lynch's moralizing of the urban aesthetic met Paley's network-executive sensitivity to the popular image.[56] The moral privilege that

50   Paley et al., 27.
51   See Jonathan Barnett, *Urban Design as Public Policy* (New York: Architectural Record Books, 1974), 7–9, for a description of the circumstances that brought Barnett, Robertson, Weinstein, and Weintraub—young architecture school graduates at the time—to public service in the Lindsay Administration.
52   Paley et al., 38.
53   Paley et al., 4.
54   Kevin Lynch, *The Image of the City* (Cambridge: MIT Press, 1960), 4.
55   Lynch, 4.

56   The introduction of *The Threatened City*, in which the proto-cinematic experience of the skyline from the peripheral routes of transportation is lauded, also smacks of Lynch's influence. Lynch's 1964 addendum to *The Image of the City*, *The View from the Road* (with Donald Appleyard and John R. Myer), provides storyboards of precisely this type of proto-cinematic experience of the urban imaginary from the periphery. See Donald Appleyard, Kevin Lynch, and John R. Myer, *The View from the Road* (Cambridge: MIT Press, 1964), 3–63.

Lynch granted the directly experienced urban image in negotiating between urban subject and the city was implicitly extended to encompass the mediated image as well—Paley's area of expertise. This media model helps explain Paley's contributions as chairman of the taskforce. Who better to gauge the possibility for positive spectatorial reactions to the mediated city than a network television executive with one eye on the city and one eye on his Nielson ratings?

Further, Paley's financial interest in grooming the image of the city cannot be ignored. In a sense, the executive was suggesting manipulations of the set that his own network planned to use for major motion pictures in the near future. Indeed, in the years following Paley's appointment to the taskforce, two of CBS's first three feature-length films were shot in Manhattan: *Me, Natalie* (1969) and *April Fools* (1969). Especially in the latter, the way Manhattan is presented to the spectator bears striking similarities to some of the visual experiences of New York suggested within *The Threatened City.*

In *April Fools,* the skyline view of the city that the taskforce lauded for its ability to establish a relationship between the individual and the city is used as a filmic technique to establish and reestablish the protagonist's presence in New York. The film begins with the camera panning along the reflective façade of a glass office tower before settling on an establishing shot of a broad Manhattan street that dead-ends into an expansive skyline view beyond. In the middle distance, a man in a gray suit paces in front of a building before being met by the protagonist and passing inside. The scene establishes the narrative within New York and provides a recurrent street and skyline image that indicates the protagonist's spatial locale within the city. Another notable scene occurs as the protagonist is returning to the city from a trip to the suburbs. On a bridge entering Manhattan, the camera affords the film viewer a shot of the protagonist in a car, followed by a long take of the city skyline beyond. Because the previous scenes were set outside of the city, the filmmakers used the skyline scenographic to resituate the narrative, protagonist, and spectator within New York. In still another scene, the protagonist is reestablished within the city against the reflection of the skyline in a Central Park pond (figs. 4-5).

Certainly, the use of the skyline establishing shot described here is not unique—it is a common technique that might be found in dozens of films contemporary or prior to *April Fools.* However, the appearance of the urban vistas suggested in *The Threatened City* as narrative devices in *April Fools* (and other films) confirms the mediatic nature of the Taskforce's urban design suggestions. Consciously or not, the taskforce forwarded design recommendations that would be both beneficial to those seeking to structure media narratives in New York, and to an urban subject whose expectations of the city

Stuart Rosenberg. *April Fools*, 1969. Frame enlargement.

were prefigured by media—whose visual navigation within the city had become analogous to the cinema spectator's visual comprehension of filmic narratives.

Films produced by Paley's company also had financial implications for the city. Positive audience reactions to films CBS made in New York (a city now designed to be cinematic) would net revenues for CBS that could be used to make more films in the city. These productions would net tax revenues for New York, and these funds, in turn, could be reinserted into planning policies that figured the city through various mediatic registers. Meanwhile, the circulation of location-shot New York City film and television productions, in which the techniques of representing the city were now

Stuart Rosenberg. *April Fools*, 1969. Frame enlargement.

coincidental with the city as shaped by urban design policy, would work to affect the associations and expectations that spectators in New York and elsewhere granted the city's built environment. The apparatus expanded.

Plan for New York City

In 1965 the photographer Charles Harbutt was included in an exhibition at New York's Museum of Modern Art titled *The Photo Essay*.[57] As the first exhibition at MOMA dedicated to the photo essay as a form, the show was a watershed moment in its definition as distinct medium. Harbutt was a member of the prestigious photojournalism cooperative *Magnum* and was featured prominently in the exhibition. The photographer's contribution was a photo essay (or, "picture story," in Harbutt's terms) titled *Blind Boys*. The piece chronicled the lives of two sightless boys, one black and one white, their interactions with one another and their surroundings, and their internal emotions and conflicts. *Blind Boys* was later published in *Contemporary Photographer*, along with a written essay by Harbutt, "The Multi-Level Picture Story."[58] In the latter, Harbutt explains some of the thought behind his piece in the MOMA show, writing: "This is a particular kind of picture story that meets all the requirements of the simple picture story form and of the needs of journalism to give information, yet somehow transcends to tell 'stories' on a deeper level."[59] As an example of Harbutt's Multi-Level Picture Story, *Blind Boys* was meant to seduce affect, convey symbolism and allegory, communicate character development, structure complex temporal and narrative relationships between images through layout design, and offer the editorial perspective of the author—all without disrupting the rote transfer of information to the viewer that Harbutt felt was fundamental to the journalistic picture story as a medium.

Concurrently on view at MOMA was the well-know exhibit *The Responsive Eye*. The show is best remembered for its explication of the "Op art" of Bridget Riley, Julian Stanczak, Victor Vasarely, and others. Op art is often characterized by visual and optical distortions through modulations of pattern and color so intense so as to produce physical reactions from viewers. The curator of *The Responsive Eye*, William C. Seitz, wrote of the pieces in the exhibit, "these works exist less as objects to be examined than as generators

57   "The Photo Essay Exhibition," The Museum of Modern Art, press release, March 15, 1965, on the MOMA website, www.moma.org/docs/press_archives/3450/releases/MOMA_1965_0026_23.pdf?2010, accessed May 1, 2013. Curated by the museum's Director of the Department of Photography, John Szarkowski, the exhibit's press re-lease boasted that it featured "four decades of experiment in a new medium."

58   Charles Harbutt, "The Multi-Level Picture Story," *Contemporary Photographer*, vol. V., no. 3 (1966), 10–12.

59   Harbutt, 10.

of perceptual responses to the eye and mind of the viewer."[60] Reaction to the exhibit transcended the art world into popular culture. One might say that the exhibit literally and figuratively hit a nerve within a society that was becoming newly aware of the cultural prominence of visuality. Television journalist Mike Wallace starred in a documentary about the exhibit for CBS. Early in the documentary, Wallace quips with a direct gaze and nod to the camera, "Who owns the responsive eye? You do." (figs. 6-7).

The co-presence of these two exhibits at MOMA is a telling condensation of emerging cultural attitudes towards the mediations of imagery at the time. In each exhibit, there is a heightened awareness of the ability of the image to solicit affect, emotion and even physical response. The pieces in each exhibit engage the viewer in order to finish the work. The images work *through* their audience. Such an attitude towards the mediations of imagery was also present in another Charles Harbutt project soon after *The Photo Essay*, as the photographer found himself in the employment of the New York City Planning Commission.

Mayor Lindsay appointed Donald H. Elliott to chair the New York City Planning Commission in 1966. An attorney, Elliott had prior served as counsel for Lindsay during his campaign. With his title the new chair inherited a foreboding mandate. The city was without a master plan, which was long absent, but required by the City Charter. More pressing yet, without a master plan the city would soon lose federal funding from the U.S. Department of Housing and Urban Development. These funds were used for programs such as Model Cities and federal urban renewal—programs New York could ill-afford to lose within its tenuous financial situation. A pragmatist, Elliott knew well that he needed to guide the Planning Commission towards the completion of a plan before the deadline. He also knew well that the city and its public were loath to accept precisely the kind of top-down governmental model of which a master plan was emblematic. The Chairman's clever negotiation of these two seemingly contradictory facts produced a remarkable document, the 1969 *Plan for New York City*.

To serve as editor of the *Plan*, Elliott hired a long-time acquaintance, Peter S. Richards. The latter was a political journalist who came to New York to work on the *Plan* from Boston, where he was a reporter for the public television station WGBH. Beyond the sensibility Richards may have brought from his television background, he was hired with a mandate to ensure that the *Plan* would be understandable to a broad public audience. The document was not to be

Part 1

60   "The Responsive Eye Exhibition," The Museum of Modern Art, press release, February 23, 1965, on the MOMA website, www.moma.org/docs/press_archives/3439/releases/MOMA_1965_0015_14.pdf?2010, accessed May 1, 2013.

CBS Television. *The Responsive Eye*, 1965. Frame enlargement.

riddled with technical planning jargon—it was meant to be plainly legible to the people of New York. To assist in this goal, William H. Whyte was brought on as a consultant to substantially edit and rewrite a first draft of the *Plan*.[61] Now well known for his work on urbanism, at the time Whyte was best known for his 1956 indictment of American corporate culture, *The Organization Man*.[62] The book is

CBS Television. *The Responsive Eye*, 1965. Frame enlargement.

61   See Richard Reeves, "Final Master Plan Draft Stirs Dispute in City Hall," *The New York Times,* October 5, 1969.

62   Whyte was also known for his contributions to the collection of essays *The Exploding Metropolis*, which also included essays by Jane Jacobs, Francis Bello, and others. Published in 1958, the book's essays discuss the declining state of American cities, suburbanization, and other urban issues from the time. See: *The Exploding Metropolis* (Garden City, New York: Doubleday, 1958). By the time Whyte was asked to work on the *Plan for New York City,* he had also very recently published his book *The Last Landscape*. The latter is a book about American urbanization with several ideological affinities with the *Plan for New York City,* suggesting that Whyte was in fact much more than an editor on the *Plan*. See: William H. Whyte, *The Last Landscape* (New York: Doubleday and Company, 1968).

noteworthy for its description of the subjectivity of the post-war sub-
urbanite, and for Whyte's agility in conveying his interests in this
sophisticated topic through accessible language. This appointment
was the beginning of a rich period of involvement in New York City
planning and urban design for Whyte, some of which will be discussed in a later chapter of this book. As picture editor—coordina-
tor of the photography that is the most striking feature of the *Plan*—
Charles Harbutt was hired. When asked to work on the *Plan*, *The
Photo Essay* had recently closed at MOMA, and Harbutt was editing
a book of Magnum photographs titled *America In Crisis*. The book
treated many of the elements of social and political unrest within
American culture that afflicted New York at the time.[63] The blend
of the sensibilities and experiences of these *Plan* team members
proved formative of the resultant document.

The *Plan for New York City* is a six-volume tome, with one book
for each of New York's boroughs and an introductory volume titled
Critical Issues (fig. 8). Each book measures 17 square inches. Opening
with a width of nearly three feet, the *Plan* creates an immersive experience for the reader. Clearly, the Planning Commission intended
to make a statement through the physical presence of the document
alone.

It would be difficult, and unnecessary for the present discussion, to summarize all of the content in the vast *Plan*. Indeed, such
a task would be complicated by the nature of the document itself.
Drafted after the fall of Robert Moses, in a time of deep suspicion
of top-down planning models, the *Plan for New York City* was a master plan that eschewed master planning. Much of the document
reads like an inventory of initiatives or policies that the Planning
Commission had already begun to implement, or that had been previously drafted in detail.[64] For example, the *Plan* includes a substantial section on the development of lower Manhattan, including
an early scheme of Battery Park City. But this content was drawn
from the 1966 *Lower Manhattan Plan*, which was drafted while William Ballard was Chairman of the Planning Commission.[65] Elsewhere, the *Plan* aspires towards ideas that seem prescient from
today's vantage, such as a recommendation to open up the city's

1

Part

63   Mitchel Levitas, *America in Crisis* (New York: Holt,
      Rinehart and Winston, 1969).
64   A draft of the *Plan* which was made available to
      city officials early in 1969 reportedly contained
      more original content, much of it more akin to so-
      cial engineering than physical planning. For exam-
      ple, the draft called for 1.9 billion dollars in aid to
      the poor, 500 million dollars in new aid to schools,
      and 500 million dollars to improve the city's
      health care infrastructure. See Richard Reeves,
      "New Master Plan Outlines Wide Social Changes
      Here," *The New York Times*, February 3, 1969. Ma-
      ny of these initiatives were removed from the *Plan*

      by the time the final draft, which was edited by
      William Whyte, was released later in 1969. Spec-
      ulation at the time was that changes were made
      because such ambitious gestures to aid the poor
      would alienate the city's white middle class, which
      was already leaving the city. See Richard Reeves,
      "Final Master Plan Draft Stirs Dispute in City Hall,"
      The New York Times, October 5, 1969.
65   The 1966 Lower Manhattan Plan was contracted
      to the firm of Wallace, McHarg, Todd, and Roberts.
      See Carol Willis ed., *The Lower Manhattan Plan:
      The 1966 Vision for Downtown New York* (New
      York: Princeton Architectural Press, 2002).

waterfront for public occupation and a provocation to build parks atop abandoned railway lines.[66] These kinds of ambitions are often presented without substantive analysis or design. And still elsewhere, the *Plan* is a purely aspirational document—thick with soaring language that reads like an assemblage of campaign promises, transcending matters of the built environment to treat the city's urban issues at large. The scopophilic concentration on urban image so clear in *The Threatened City* is present in the *Plan*. The document reiterates an insistence on the importance of scenic vistas and advocates "visual review" by the city of private development plans.[67] But, such suggestions are less prominent in the *Plan* than in *The Threatened City*.

Even before its release, rumors of the *Plan's* content were the subject of controversy.[68] After its release, the *Plan's* critics became more pointed.[69] Most outspoken was planning commissioner Beverly

fig.
8

The six-volume *Plan for New York City.*

66   While these suggestions may seem prescient, they are not without ideology. Theorists of the political economy of cities have noted that movements like those to open formerly working waterfronts or railways for public occupation are symptomatic of inter-urban competition in post-industrial economies in order to combat the nimble and fleeting urbanization of flexible accumulation. According to this critique, the real goal of such "public space" initiatives is to make cities more competitive for consumers and business. In this scenario, elite corporate interests are best served, while those of the dwindling working class are worst served. See, for example David Harvey, "Flexible Accumulation through Urbanization Reflections on 'Post-Modernism' in the American City," *Perspecta*, vol. 26 (1990): 251–272.

67   Elliott, *Critical Issues*, 22.

68   See Robert E. Tomasson, "City Master Plan Must be Released," *The New York Times*, November 4, 1969.

69   See the *Journal of the American Institute of Planners* XXXVI, no. 6 (November 1970): 436–449, for a series of reviews of the 1969 *Plan*. In that issue, critics including Ada Louis Huxtable, Beverly Moss Spatt, Sigurd Grava, Paul Niebanck, and Marcia Marker Feld contribute to the opinion that the 1969 *Plan*, while sometimes ambitious in its suggestions, was lacking in substantive analysis and detailed plans for execution.

Moss Spatt. Noting the document had been written by Elliott and
his exclusive team, Spatt called the *Plan* a "letter to Santa Claus."
The Commissioner's criticisms revolve around the lack of function-
al specificity and benchmarks for implementation in the *Plan's* content.[70] Spatt wrote that the *Plan* "derides any professional attempt
to establish long range goals and programs based on critical analysis, demographic projections, economic data and technical studies."[71] Assessed in comparison to a typical master plan and typical
planning practices, Spatt's criticisms are perhaps sound. Indeed,
the *Plan* is not a technical document. But the creators of the 1969
Plan had no intention of producing a typical master plan. Early in
the document, the authors of the *Plan* state:

> The *Plan* is not a conventional master plan. It is not,
> for one thing, primarily a physical plan. While we do
> go into considerable detail on many construction and
> public works projects, our purpose is not to present
> an over-all design for physical development. Put on
> colored maps, such plans do present a nice sense of or-
> der, but one which does not have too much to do with
> *reality.* Our primary concern is with the *process* for the
> City's growth . . . We have not made elaborate trend
> projections, nor have we specified phase one and
> phase two goals or any ultimate grand design. This
> would be paper boldness. It would also be intellectu-
> ally presumptuous. Our plans are going to be influ-
> enced by forces that the City can neither forecast nor
> control.[72]

Faced with such a disclosure of reduced expectations, one might
question what, precisely, the *Plan's* authors intended to accomplish
through their document. If not the physical city, what exactly was
the *Plan* planning?

  As its authors admit, the intended product of the *Plan* was not
the physical city—not *directly.* Rather, the product was meant to be
a new kind of citizen. The *Plan* is a complexly interwoven combination of text, graphics and, *most prominently*, images. The document
is best understood as a kind of *cool* media that sought to establish
an audience for planning policy, and to galvanize that audience as a
tuned-in citizenry of the city.[73] It is this discursive motion *through*

Part 1

70   Elliott, *Critical Issues,* 174.
71   Elliott, *Critical Issues,* 174. See Beverly Moss Spatt,
     *A Proposal to Change the Structure of City Plan-
     ning; Case Study of New York City* (New York:
     Praeger, 1971), 39–48, for a more complete sum-
     mary of the commissioner's dissentions from the
     1969 *Plan for New York City.*
72   Elliott, *Critical Issues,* 6.

73   Marshall McLuhan has defined a cool medium as
     one that is low-definition, vague in its message,
     and therefore solicitous of participation on behalf
     of its recipient. I use McLuhan's term here primar-
     ily for the latter half of his definition. The *Plan for
     New York City* was understood to be solicitous of
     public engagement in order to finish its work. See
     Marshall McLuhan, *Understanding Media: The
     Extensions of Man* (New York: MIT Press, 1994),
     22–32.

the public-as-audience, and through issues of economy and policy detailed in the *Plan's* text, that explains the authors' interest in the "*process* for the City's growth."[74] And it is the experiences and subject positions of the citizens (a citizenry now conceptually elided with the media audience) that more fully satisfied the authors' notion of *reality* than projections of the city's abstract physical presence. With its release, the authors of the *Plan* implicitly turned to the public and quipped with a nod: "Who owns the *Plan for New York City?* You do."

The *Critical Issues* volume of the *Plan* is exemplary of the way in which the document sought to operate as media through its audience. In the introduction of the volume, the authors establish themes that are pervasive throughout the *Plan*. Using language that recalls the proclamation in *The Threatened City* that "New York emits, the nation receives," the authors advocate further development in what they term "The National Center"—a phrase referring to the combined business districts of Midtown and Lower Manhattan, and punctuating the importance of these areas as radiators of culture and economy. However, the *Plan's* authors understood that further development in Midtown would heighten already choking congestion and crowding and would therefore be unpopular among citizens. Stridently, the authors persuade: "But concentration is the genius of the City, its reason for being, the source of its *vitality* and its excitement. We believe the center should be strengthened, not weakened, and we are not afraid of the bogey man of density."[75] Similarly, the *Plan* later celebrates the urban dynamics resultant from density in the National Center as the impetus of everything that "makes a city jump and hum with *life* . . ." calling such dynamism "the ancient rhythms of the City."[76] Such ebulliently anthropomorphic language initiates the recurrent trope of naturalizing the city's dynamics, describing New York as a kind of quasi-organic entity whose ecological processes are an object of near sublime wonder. In what might seem an attempt to tame such sublimity, the authors then initiate another recurrent trope, offering "Our hope for the *Plan* is that it will help give them (the people of New York) good choices to make," and later ". . . we think the main requirement is that it makes sense to the citizens of the City. It is written for them, and their judgment of it will help determine what is to become of it."[77] Conjoining these two reoccurring themes is a single latent concept: the city is an intricately intertwined ecology of matter, systems and citizens, and it is *through the citizen* that planning might find agency in effecting the city's processes.[78]

74   Elliott, *Critical Issues*, 6.
75   Elliott, *Critical Issues*, 5. Emphasis added.
76   Elliott, *Critical Issues*, 5. Emphasis added.
77   Elliott, *Critical Issues*, 5.

Turning the massive page from the introductory text, the method through which the *Plan* was meant to work through its audience becomes clear, as the viewer is met with four enigmatic images. Visually complex, these images overtly solicit interpretation, requiring the viewer to participate in their decoding (fig. 9). The first is a surreal registration of triangular zones of shadow and light; reflection and refraction, within which vaguely familiar forms of skyscrapers and curtain walls fade in and out of legibility. The second depicts two boys sitting in an unknown empty field, their faces concealed in shadow with the Statue of Liberty in the background. The third is another jumble of shadow and reflection, with an anonymous man in black hat and suit, his face concealed, apparently descending in a diagonal across the composition. Finally, the fourth depicts a pond (in Central Park?) within which the surrounding buildings cast rippling reflections, while in the corner a young girl, her back turned to the camera, points to the image (figs. 10-13). In each photograph, the city is something to be *augured*. It is undefined, too confusing to be immediately apprehended. The photographs beg contemplative engagement with the viewer. The people depicted in each image are concealed to maintain their anonymity. Thus, they become

1

Part

fig.
9

Introductory image spread from the *Plan for New York City*.

78   Lindsay's Planning Commission can be characterized by a growing level of environmental, cultural, and urban ecological awareness. The section of *Critical Issues* titled "Environment" reflects this fact, as does other documents produced for the Commission such as Lawrence Halprin's *New York, New York* (Lawrence Halprin, *New York, New York* (San Francisco: Chapman Press, 1968), a report commissioned by the city with federal grant money. The Commission's interest in ecology was probably made most evident in a conference titled *Restructuring The Ecology of a Great City*, which was hosted by the Wenner-Gren Foundation for Anthropological Research, Inc., in New York on October 26–31, 1970. The conference was conceived by Jaquelin Robertson, Director of the Office for Midtown Planning and Development, and was organized by Gregory Bateson. For a transcript of Bateson's comments at the conference, see Gregory Bateson, "Ecology and Flexibility in Urban Civilization," in *Steps to an Ecology of Mind* (Chicago: University of Chicago Press, 1972), 502–513. This conference is discussed in further detail in Part 2, Chapter III of this book. The contention here is that these ideas about ecology, perhaps unconsciously, infiltrated the way in which the commission understood the city, the role of planning and physical design, and the urban subject's intercourse with the urban environment.

fig.
10

Skyscraper reflected in office window. Ernst Haas.

fig.
11

Statue of Liberty. Bruce Davidson.

less individuals than generic types through which the viewer may more easily identify, and project him or herself. Viewed immediately after the introductory text, the effects of the images are multiplied. If the reader harbored some predetermined vision of the density and dynamics that the *Plan's* authors advocated, these images seem placed to prompt a radical rethinking of those expectations. If the text insisted that the *Plan* work through the city's citizens, the introductory images reaffirm that point by demanding an analytic mentality of their audience.

fig.
12

Reflection in Central Park Lake. Bruce Davidson.

fig.
13

Park Avenue office building. Charles Harbutt.

The pages immediately following exploit the erasure of expectation
effected by the introduction images, beginning to tune the audience
to a *new* way of understanding the city. The proceeding eight pages
comprise four image spreads, each a brief picture essay. The first
spread is accompanied by a William Shakespeare quote: "What Is
the city but the people?"[79] (fig. 14). The accompanying images affirm
that the question is rhetorical by representing the city as a dense
aggregation of individuals. In the upper left is a large photo, taken
from a high vantage, of citizens on the boardwalk and beach at

79   This is a quotation from Shakespeare's *Coriola-
      nus*. The line, from Act III, Scene I, is spoken by Si-
      cinius in reference to Rome.

Coney Island. The photograph depicts a crowd, but the white surface of the sand and the gray of the boardwalk objectify each individual in stark contrast against a common background (fig. 15). The
astute viewer might surmise some analogical relationship to the city
itself. The surrounding photographs then deliver a cross-section of
urban subjectivities existent within the city (and presumably within this photo of Coney Island): a young mother and daughter on
the steps of a brownstone, a group of Chinese restaurant workers, a
businessman, a dancer, a group of hard-scrabbled children on a city
street, and more (figs. 16-20). As is often the case throughout the *Plan*,
the message approaches didacticism. Like the crowd on the white
sandy beach, the city is a dense interaction of activity, composed of
individual citizens.

    This message is then elaborated on the follow image spread,
one accompanied by another quote, this time from Marcus Aurelius:
"Whatever is in any way beautiful hath its source in beauty itself…"[80]
(fig. 21). Below the quote is an array of photographs depicting aestheticized effects of urban density and ecological dynamics—the flows
and quasi-organic aspects of the city the authors of the *Plan* were so
keen to celebrate. Prominent among these images is an aerial view
of Washington Square Monument in the winter. Vacant except for
a single individual, the surrounding snow is marked with long arcs
from vehicular traffic and a swarm of footprints (fig. 22). The viewer is
meant to decipher patterns from the indexes of dense urban interaction, and per Aurelius, deem them "beautiful." The remaining images convey similar messages. One shows a vaguely cubist aggregation of Greenwich Village rooftops, apparent real-estate carbuncles
adhered as if by nature to the flow of capital. Another two images depict street traffic flowing in the rain, the motion of cars conceptually elided to, and literally saturated with, the perpendicular flow of
rain. In these images, the pavement moodily reflects patterns from
the surrounding lights and activities, conveying a thick affect of the
atmospheric (figs. 23-24). Preceding these images is another, depicting
a group of birdwatchers in Central Park (fig. 25). This image seems
placed to instruct the viewer on his / her role. The birdwatchers are
presumably extracting views of the park the likes of the surrounding
photographs in this image spread. Here, the parks stands in for the
city as an analogical "wilderness"; the "natural" standing in for the
naturalized.

    The following two spreads continue to develop the *Plan's*
recurring concepts that the city is a sublimely organized system
or ecology, and that this organization is composed of participatory individuals. Throughout these introductory pages, the *Plan's*
images are meant to work through the viewer on several levels.

80   Marcus Aurelius, *Meditations. iv. 10.*

Image spread from the *Plan for New York City*.

fig.
14

Coney Island beach. Andreas Feininger.

fig.
15

Brownstone stoop in Brookyn Heights. Charles Harbutt.

fig.
16

fig.
17

Cooks in a Chinatown restaurant.
Maggie Sherwood.

fig.
18

1

Part

Outside a movie house. Charles Harbutt.

fig.
19

Modern dance studio in Manhattan. Victor Laredo.

East Harlem children. Helen Levitt.

Image spread from the *Plan for New York City*.

fig. 21

fig. 22

Washington Square. Andre Kertesz.

fig. 23

Greenwich Village rooftops. Andre Kertesz.

fig. 24

Festival of Saint Gennaro. Bruce Davidson.

fig.
25

Birdwatchers in Central Park. Sam Falk.

One is prompted to apprehend the *Plan's* overarching themes, to piece together a message from a collection of images operating together, to be affected by details such as concealed faces, to assign symbolic or analogic value to elements like footprints in the snow, and more. Indeed, the introduction exposes the viewer to the full panoply of communication and affect through imagery that Charles Harbutt called the "multi-level picture story." Further, the text and imagery work together in a calculated way. In the introduction, ideas are established in the text, then punctuated, elaborated, or rethought through the imagery. This establishes a complex interrelation between text and image that is pervasive throughout *Plan's* content. Thus, the introduction and image essays, taken together, tutor the *Plan's* audience on the modes of literacy and sensibility required for the remainder of the document, and, by extension, for life in the city.

Progressing into the body of *Critical Issues*, the orientation that the *Plan's* audience received in the introduction is put to use. The volume is structured under headings titled National Center, Opportunity, Environment, and Government. What the authors meant by National Center has already been stated.[81] The Opportunity section addresses the need for jobs, education, and related issues.[82] The Environment section addresses issues of the built environment, such as housing, as well as those springing from the burgeoning ecological awareness of the time.[83] Finally, the Government section addresses

---

81   Elliott, *Critical Issues*, 24–57.   83   Elliott, *Critical Issues*, 108–161.
82   Elliott, *Critical Issues*, 58–107.

issues of policy and finance required to actuate the ideas forwarded in the sections preceding.[84]

Significantly, each section brackets and hosts a discourse rather than succinctly delivering information related to discrete subjects. For example, in the Opportunity section a discussion about industrial jobs quickly segues to related issues of land use, to a visionary suggestion for the development of vertical factory typologies, to immediate issues of social unrest among the city's minorities, and so on. Affirming the author's stated interest in process and their celebration of the city as a quasi-organic entity, each of the *Plan's* topics are discussed as a function of their ecological motion through the various inputs and outputs, interests and objections, by which they are defined.

Each section in *Critical Issues* is presented with two lengthy picture essays, one at the beginning treating the past and one near the end treating the present. Combined, each pair of essays delivers a thesis building upon the *Plan's* larger ideological objectives. In the section of the *Plan* discussing the National Center, the picture essays elide street-level flow and density with technological exchange, allying both with the city's production of cultural capital. The essay treating the National Center's past includes an array of historic woodcut prints and illustrations of the ways in which New York has served as a cultural and business center for the nation (fig. 26). The essay begins with an image of Broadway in the 19th century, densely crowded with pedestrians (fig. 27). Following this is an illustration of Lower Manhattan shipyards in 1869, with goods flowing in and out (fig. 28). One picture spread later is an image of an early 20th century brokerage house complete with ticker-tape machine, and later an image of an 18th century telephone exchange room (figs. 29-30). Various historic images of the arts within the city follow in another spread (fig. 31). The picture essay treating the then-present of the National Center anchors the conclusion to the section. A spread of photographs portraying urban density and flow includes an image of congestion on 5th Avenue, as well a tightly cropped photograph of commuters packed on conveyor-belt-like Port Authority escalators (figs. 32-34). Two spreads later, the viewer is shown an image of a master control room at NBC and a similar control room at a network radio station—the multitude of circular dials and buttons upon the controls perhaps evoking the memory of heads aligned on the Port Authority escalators (figs. 35-36). Finally, the essay presents a page of images depicting the city's arts production (fig. 37). Among these: a solitary painter gazing reflectively at his canvas, a dancer's torso emerging from shadows with one arm reaching for the sky, and an orchestra rehearsal with members circled around the conductor (figs. 38-40).

84   Elliott, *Critical Issues*, 162–173.

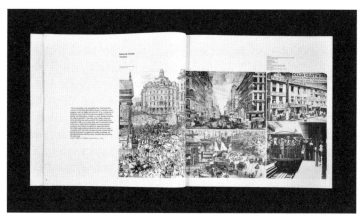

Image spread from the *Plan for New York City*.

fig. 26

fig. 27

Traffic jam on Broadway, c. 1870.

Part 1

West Street, 1869.

fig.
28

Brokerage House, c. 1910.

fig.
29

fig.
30

New York telephone exchange, 1880.

1

Part

fig.
31

Image spread from the *Plan for New York City*.

Image spread from the *Plan for New York City.*

Fifth Avenue at noon, 1955.
Andreas Feininger.

fig.
32

fig.
33

fig.
34

Port Authority bus terminal. Louis B. Schlivek.

fig.
35

Network radio master control room. Erich Hartmann.

1

Part

NBC Master control. Erich Hartmann.

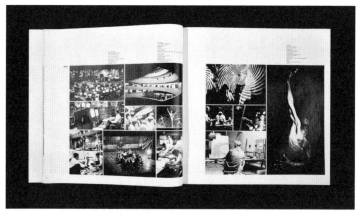

Image spread from the *Plan for New York City.*

William de Kooning in his Manhattan studio. Dan Budnik.

fig.
37

fig.
38

Modern dancer Charles Moore. Peter Fink.

fig.
39

Igor Stravinsky rehearsing. Dennis Stock.

fig.
40

Throughout both picture essays, the images are presented in black and white, in a consistent, adjustable image grid, and with controlled tones that dapple each spread, unifying the two essays into alternating fields of light and dark. Such unifying aesthetics aids in the messaging. Across the temporal settings depicted, individuals on congested city streets or escalators are visually compared to mechanical dials, buttons or ticker tape machine gears. They are, alike, participatory singularities within vast, dynamic surrounding systems—singularities within their surrounding ecologies. And the essay visually alludes that culture is also systemically produced within the city's confines. The products of the painter, the dancer and the orchestra all pulse outward from the city in mechanized rhythm. Their flows intertwine with those of the dynamic crowds and technological devices depicted in pages preceding, all part of the city's kinetic urban ecology.

Between the two photo essays is the section's text. Here, the *Plan's* authors advocate development that would amplify precisely the characteristics of the National Center treated in the picture essays—its kinesis, and density with activities that radiate out to affect the nation's culture and economy. For example, the text discusses a plan by the Office of Midtown Planning and Development to radically increase density in West Midtown through the construction of a mixed-use development.[85] The scheme featured sectionally layered infrastructure of pedestrian and vehicular traffic that would seem to multiply possibilities of complex interaction (fig. 41). Later, the Planning Commission's initiative to save and expand the Midtown theatre district is discussed. Historically a cultural asset to the city, the *Plan* cited the Commission's recent incentive zoning program to entice developer investment in the area.[86] By preceding these planning suggestions with a picture essay of historic images, the *Plan's* authors seem intent on seducing a nostalgic sentiment from the reader and portraying the characteristics of the National Center that the *Plan's* suggestions build upon as objects of nostalgic reflection that are pervasive within the city's past to the point of naturalization. The picture essay of the present works to associate familiar scenes from the reader's daily reality with the narrative running through the essay of the past and the *Plan's* text. The reader is prompted to understand these aspects of his / her daily interaction with the city as part of a teleology that makes the *Plan's* proposals seem nearly inevitable.

The remaining sections of *Critical Issues* are structured similarly, with text separating picture essays in order to establish rich relationships between and across. As in the introduction, these relationships overtly invite decoding by their audience. To be sure, such solicitation to interpretation assumes a high level of visual literacy.

85   Elliott, *Critical Issues*, 34.   86   Elliott, *Critical Issues*, 32–33.

fig. 41

Proposed 48th Street transportation corridor.

Perhaps the *Plan* was meant to elevate its audience to this erudite level, its authors deeming such an education appropriate for their contemporary urban culture. Or perhaps the intended effect of the *Plan* was less cerebral and more subliminal—with messages burnt into the consciousness of its audience like a retinal after-image. Regardless, the images build upon well-establish theoretical trajectories for photographic representation. The use of imagery in the *Plan* to capture fleeting moments of urban dynamics that are invisible to the naked eye extends a tradition spanning from the 19th century experimentation of Eadweard Muybridge and Etienne-Jules Marey through Susan Sontag's characterization of the photograph as a "neat slice of time."[87] The *Plan's* evident faith in the potential of the photographic medium to reproduce images of urban "reality" engages a theoretical discourse populated by Andre Bazin, Roland Barthes, and others.[88] The placement of photographs leveraging these traditions within the picture essay form has been less theorized. Much more recently, W.J.T. Mitchell has written about photographic essays, highlighting the medium's potential to establish critically recursive relationships between text and image.[89] Notwithstanding the complex text to image relationships in the *Plan*, the document's photographic essays, and the way these essays deploy narrative through imagery, seem to belong to another paradigm—one perhaps more properly described as proto-cinematic or proto-televisual. This assessment is supported through analysis of the borough volumes of the *Plan*.

Each borough volume is divided into several sections by city neighborhood, and each section contains a dense collection of images,

87 Susan Sontag, "In Plato's Cave," in *On Photography* (New York: Farrar, Straus and Giroux, 1977), 17.

88 See, for example, Andre Bazin (trans. Hugh Gray), "The Ontology of the Photographic Image," *Film Quarterly*, vol. 13, no. 4 (Summer, 1960), 4–9 and Roland Barthes, *Camera Lucida: Reflections on Photography* (New York: Farrar, Straus and Giroux, 1980).

89 In his own words, Mitchell's interest is in "...the kinds of photographic essays which contain strong textual elements, where the text is most definitely an "invasive" and almost domineering element." See W.J.T. Mitchell, *Picture Theory: Essays on Verbal and Visual Representation* (Chicago: University of Chicago Press, 1995), 286.

with text woven between under the recurrent headings of population, neighborhood character, institutions, industry, shopping, and recreations. The text is consistent with that in *Critical Issues*—ranging from moments of aspirational tone, to recapitulations of existing initiatives. More remarkable is the structural arrangement and content of the imagery. The section of the Manhattan volume covering Midtown is exemplary.

Above the section's text, a dramatic series of black-and-white photographs dominates the entire top half of each page. The photographs capture fleeting impressions of city life (figs. 42-43). One image portrays a couple appearing startled on a city street—framed at the lower left corner of the shot, and staring off at an undepicted event (fig. 44). The viewer wonders what caused the couple's alarm in the moment before the photograph was taken (what is the couple staring at?) and wonders what happened in the moment after the photograph was shot. Another photograph depicts the neon glare of a 46th Street bar, with a car captured partially in the frame while driving by (fig. 45). Groups of people seated at tables inside the bar are barely visible through the storefront windows. The viewer is invited to wonder what kinds of stories might be taking place within the bar between the vaguely visible New Yorkers. What brought these individuals to this point in the city, and what will happen next? The passing car, only partially captured in the frame, indexes a temporality that makes the shot, paradoxically, more allied to the moving image than photography—we know that in the instance before the shot was taken, the car was outside of the frame to the left and that in the instance after, the car will be off the frame to the right. Hence, each photograph is infused with a narrative and temporality that begs a cinematic or televisual reading.

Still more interesting is the way in which the assemblage of photographs in this section of the *Plan* works to structure an impression *between* images. Each image is cropped to include a minimum of decipherable urban fabric. No single photograph offers a comprehensive view of the city. Rather the images depict local details and fragments—operating on the level of the synecdoche or as a montage of details to be consumed over time and in sequence (figs. 46-47). The series of photographs continues for three-and-a-half pages before ending with an aerial photograph of Midtown that fills a full half of one page (fig. 48). The effect of the aerial, read in sequence after the series of urban detail photographs, is to provide an abstraction in which to spatialize the events depicted in the detail photography. In exercising these conventions of urban representation—the synecdoche, the montage, the spatializing aerial—the *Plan* implements techniques discussed by film theorists like Sergei Eisenstein, Siegfried Kracauer, and others.[90] The use of these conventions could be dismissed as coincidental had Mayor Lindsay not already expressed

Part 1

his desire to make a film of the *Plan for New York City*. In 1969, the
mayor was granted his wish, and the film was indeed made.[91] An investigation of the movie makes clear the mediatic paradigm on which
the *Plan* was modeled.

What Is the City but the People?

On November 28, 1956, in Manhattan on the 8th floor of Ray-
mond Hood's 30 Rockefeller Center, Herbert Stempel was a contes-
tant on the NBC television quiz show *Twenty-One*. At a critical moment in the game Jack Barry, host of the program, asked Stempel
a question to which he knew the answer: What motion picture won
the academy award for 1955? The answer is *Marty*, reportedly one of
Stempel's favorite films. Stempel darted an intense glare (fig. 49). Fifty seconds later, he delivered his answer: *On the Waterfront*. The
incorrect response cost Stempel the game. The winner was Charles
Van Doren, an English professor at Columbia University and son of
the Pulitzer Prize winning poet Mark Van Doren. Stempel went on
to publicly claim that the producer of *Twenty-One*, Dan Enright, had
instructed him to answer incorrectly, throwing the game in Van
Doren's direction. Stempel was vindicated two years later when
news of the widespread rigging of the popular network television
quiz shows came to light. These events came to be known as the
"Quiz Show Scandals."

fig.
42

Image spread from the *Plan for New York City*.

90   For a theoretical discussion of synecdoche, see
      Kracauer, 45–52; and Sergei Eisenstein, "Meth-
      ods of Montage," in *Film Form: Essays in Film
      Theory*, ed. and tr. Jay Leyda, (San Diego: Har-
      court Brace and Company, 1977), 72–83. For a dis-
      cussion of the aerial as a spatializing agent, see

      Edward Dimendberg, *Film Noir and the Spaces of
      Modernity* (Cambridge, MA: Harvard University
      Press, 2004), 36–47.
91   The title is a quotation from Shakespeare's *Corio-
      lanus*. The line, from Act III, Scene I, is spoken by
      Sicinius in reference to Rome.

Image spread from the *Plan for New York City.*

Theatre District: Helen Hayes Theatre. Charles Harbutt.

Times Square. Charles Harbutt.

fig.
43

fig.
44

fig.
45

fig.
46

Grand Army Plaza reflected in department store window. Charles Harbutt.

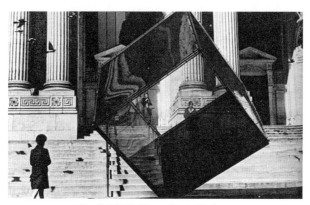

fig.
47

New York Public Library. Charles Harbutt.

Image spread from the *Plan for New York City*.

There followed an onslaught of public disenchantment and reflection on the role of network television in society. Until the scandals, the networks seemed to have a tacit contract of honesty and even-brokerage with their audience. Remarkable from our contemporary perspective, the broad public consensus at the time was that one could believe what he or she saw on television. But revelation of quiz show rigging cost the networks a significant loss of credibility in the public's eye. In an attempt to force penance for their crimes against the airways, FCC chairman John Doefer announced an initiative obliging the networks to broadcast one hour of public service television each week. While the Doefer Plan was never enforced, its sentiment proved to be influential.[92]

In the decade following, network television produced a huge swell of documentary films. Notable for their vast quantity and range of subject matter—from history, to public service announcement, to art, and more—documentary films began to draw an unprecedented number of talented filmmakers.[93] Networks were staffed with professionals with renewed faith in the television medium as a tool for public service and education. Among the many who were drawn to the documentary medium was Charles Harbutt, who made films for CBS and NBC, including a one-hour film titled *New York* for NBC in 1961.

Also drawn to documentary filmmaking was the writer, director and producer Gordon Hyatt, who is best known for his work with CBS. In the early 1960s, WCBS in New York, under William S. Paley's leadership, aired a series of documentaries about New York City's built environment. The films were titled *Our Vanishing Legacy* (1961), *Reflections on the Fair* (1964), *A Question of Values* (1964),

92   Mary Ann Watson, *The Expanding Vista: American Television in the Kennedy Years* (Durham: Duke University Press, 1994), 72.

93   Watson, 135–139.

A Fantasy of Forgotten Corners (1966), and *Cities of the Future*. Written and produced by Hyatt, the films projected visions of the New York of the future and treated contemporary issues such as urban and environmental blight. *Our Vanishing Legacy* was perhaps the most effective film of the group. An indictment of recent urban development in the city at the expense of New York's historic urban fabric, the film may have been instrumental in persuading the public to take notice of the city's urban renewal policies and the wave of unmitigated real-estate development that resulted in the early 1960s.[94] The film first aired on CBS on September 21, 1961, and was praised by the press for its attempts to win public support for landmarks preservation—years before the New York City Landmarks Law was passed in 1965.[95]

It was within this context that Mayor Lindsay agreed to make a documentary film version of the 1969 *Plan for New York City*. The WCBS films, as well as others resulting from the television documentary boom, may well have been on Mayor Lindsay's mind, or those of his advisors, when the city's film was planned. Through the WCBS productions, the mayor and his advisors may have become convinced not only that the city could be effectively represented through media

fig.
49

NBC Studios. *Twenty One*, 1956. Frame enlargement.

94   The planning commission was partially responsible for this wave of development. In 1960, after years of negotiation with real-estate interests, the commission passed a new zoning resolution to reflect decreased assessments of future population. The revision stipulated far lower maximum square footage figures for midtown lots and was poised to infuriate influential members of the New York real-estate industry. To assuage these interests, the new zoning revision allowed a one-year grace period for compliance with the new resolution. As a result, 1961 witnessed an unprecedented onslaught of submitted plans from developers intent on securing permits under the old zoning regulations. The building boom that followed dramatically changed Midtown Manhattan throughout the 1960s—robbing the city of what many later valued as a prized architectural heritage.

95   See "TV: Focus on New York," *The New York Times*, September 22, 1961.

but also that these mediated representations could modify public attitudes towards the built environment.

As recounted by Peter S. Richards, editor of the 1969 *Plan*, it was he who first recommended making a film version of the document, apparently drawing from his experience as a broadcast journalist for WGBH.[96] The film was titled *What Is the City but the People?*, again borrowing the Shakespeare quote used in the *Plan for New York City*. It was made to fill a one-hour segment on the local public television station, WNYC. The credited writer and producer was John Peer Nugent, who entered the job with some documentary writing experience and went on to write biographical books.[97] Despite this credit, most of the narration in *What Is the City but the People?* is borrowed or paraphrased directly from the *Plan*. Nugent is also credited as co-director of the film, along with Gordon Hyatt, who was known by this time for his WCBS films about New York City. The film was edited by another CBS employee, Lee Reichental. *What Is the City but the People* is narrated by William H. Whyte and stars chairman of the planning commission Donald Elliott. Prominent among the remaining credits was the cinematographer, Arthur Ornitz—a well-known Hollywood tradesman who also worked on New York City films such as *Midnight Cowboy*, *Next Stop Greenwich Village* (Mark Marzursky, 1973), and *Serpico* (Sidney Lumet, 1976). This list of players once again reinforces notions of an interpersonnel and financial symbiosis between the film industry and city planning in New York.

Arthur Ornitz's presence as a cinematographer is also indicative of an important stylistic and intellectual influence to *What Is the City but the People?* With experience on films associated with the New Hollywood movement in cinema, Ornitz brought formative aesthetic and communicative techniques to the film. New Hollywood productions often built upon experimental techniques from various cinematic avant-gardes—complex montage sequences, disjunctive editing, internalized critiques of the materiality of film, or the limits of cinema's modes of production. Such avant-garde films often took as their subject matter *how* cinema might mean, producing complex meditations on cinematic code.[98] While New Hollywood is sometimes characterized as an articulation of the moment when such avant-garde techniques were integrated, and thus sublimated, into conventional modes of cinematic production, Ornitz's aesthetic contribution to *What Is the City but the People?* nevertheless helped to create a film that sometimes stands in contrast to the norm for television documentaries at the time. However diluted, the presence of filmic

96   Peter Richards interview with the author on June
      18, 2013.
97   Among Nugent's titles are *The Black Eagle* (New
      York: Stein and Day, 1971) and *White Night* (New
      York: Rawson, Wade Publishers, 1978).

98   David E. James, *Allegories of Cinema: American
      Film in the Sixties* (Princeton: Princeton University Press, 1989), 26-27.

techniques that were meant to critique *how* cinema might mean produced a unique film that spans communicative registers from the didactic to the intensely affective.

Ornitz's contributions not withstanding, *What Is the City But the
People?* is not a cinematic masterpiece. An apparent jumble of influences and stylistic nods, the film is often plainly a commercial for the
Planning Commission's objectives. In many places, the film conveys
abridged introductions to standing or proposed planning policy in
an attempt to make these policies accessible. Elsewhere, the narration delivers moralizing and folksy wisdom that smacks of William
Whyte's voice. The broad themes of *What Is the City But the People?*
are consistent with those within the *Plan for New York City*. As in the
Plan, most prominent are the conjoined assertions that the city is a
complex quasi-organic ecology, fueled through urban density, and
that it is through the orientation of the citizen that planning may have
agency in effecting the city-as-system.

What is more singularly remarkable in *What Is the City But the
People?* is the way its broad themes are treated in a medium that is so
uniquely appropriate for their dissemination. In more effective seg-
ments of the film, and those that will be analyzed here, it is the filmic code, the visual rhetoric, that is most intensely communicative,
and not necessarily the apparent content. The density and kinesis of
the city that the authors of the *Plan* applauded as "the genius of the
City, its reason for being, the source of its vitality and its excitement,"[99] is fittingly revealed and re-presented by capturing precisely this kinesis, this movement over time, in a motion picture.[100] The
capacity of the motion picture to connect to an audience through
aesthetic techniques that might cut through cultural inattentiveness
nominates the movie as a privileged medium for the *Plan*'s author's
goals of re-presenting the city to the public through media.[101] Cinema has often been theorized as a representation of the consciousness
of the urban subject.[102] The registration of fast-paced events over
time on film has been understood as an analogue to the registration
of precisely those events—those stimuli—on the consciousness of the
individual on the street. Hence, film might play a valuable role in
re-tuning the subject positions of a city's public, as was the goal of
the *Plan*'s authors. In this light, it seems the movie was the medium
the *Plan*'s authors were assuming from the start.

99   Elliott, *Critical Issues*, 5.
100   Among others, Siegfried Kracauer has discussed
      this capacity of cinema. See Siegfried Kracauer,
      *Theory of Film: The Redemption of Physical Real-
      ity* (New York: Oxford University Press, 1965), XX.
101   Along these lines, Walter Benjamin wrote that cin-
      ema "in permitting the reproduction to meet the
      beholder or listener in his own particular situation"
      could "reactivate the object reproduced"—hence
      awakening the viewing subject from distraction
      and ideology. See Walter Benjamin, "The Work of
      Art in the Age of Mechanical Reproduction," in *Il-
      luminations* (New York: Shocken Books, 1968), 221.
102   These observations often build upon Benjamin.
      "Work of Art," 217–251. Who was, himself, building
      upon the work of Georg Simmel, "The Metropolis
      and Mental Life," in *The Sociology of Georg Sim-
      mel*, adapt. D. Weinstein, trans. Kurt Wolff (New
      York: Free Press, 1950), 409–424.

Such a statement is supported through an analysis of the introduction of *What Is the City but the People?*, a montage sequence that is a precise filmic realization of the method of image organization in the borough volumes of the *Plan for New York City*. The film begins with a panning aerial shot of Manhattan, accompanied by background audio of a helicopter's spinning propeller. It quickly becomes clear that we are meant to understand this vantage as the typical planner's conception of the city.[103] The aerial is the type of totalizing view—held far above the level of urban interaction—that allows a planner to conceive of the city as an abstraction to be formally ordered. From above, we can read the rigid metering of the city blocks and the uniform shapes of the buildings within. The aerial shot changes several times, showing different parts of the city and different versions of formal order: densely gridded city blocks, a uniform cluster of pre-1962 zoning towers, and the sort of modernist towers within a field that are characteristic of urban renewal. Montaged between these different visions of order are depictions of kinetic, disruptive, and often violent detail events within the city. We are shown a crumbling storefront with rubble piled in front, quick shots of signs delivering messages like "danger," "warning," and "sex," a man and woman fighting on a city street, a few seconds of a protest scene, a broken window, a spinning police siren, and more (figs. 50-64). Accompanying these quick shots are the sounds of angry mobs, protests, traffic jams, and other audio samples of urban unrest. The montaged shots starkly contrast the seemingly formally ordered New York with the disjunctive problems within the city that occur on the level of human interaction.

This scene's rhetoric problematizes the typical planner's vision of the city and critiques the impulse to understand the city as an abstraction. The film implies that the various formal organizations that have been imposed on the city (which are most visible from the abstracting aerial view) are speciously simple and do little to resolve the actual planning problems of New York. The use of montage reveals the limitations of conceiving of the city as an abstraction by foiling the aerial against the violent detail events, which the film's rhetoric implies depict the *real* planning problems in the city. These problems occur on the level of the urban subject, to whom the city appears disjunctive, syncopated, and montaged.[104] On the level of

103 See John R. Gold and Stephen Ward, "Of Plans and Planners: Documentary Film and the Challenge of the Urban Future, 1935-1952," in *The Cinematic City*, ed. David B. Clarke, (London: Routledge, 1997), 59-82.

104 The structure of this introductory scene, with detail events in the city montaged against the aerial view, bears striking resemblance to the introductory scene to Jules Dassin's 1948 film noir, *The Naked City*. Dassin's introductory scene even features the sound of the helicopter propeller in the soundtrack (as does the planning commission's film). In 1948, Dassin's film was quite remarkable for its insistence on location shooting; it was the first film to do so in such volume in twenty-two years. As in *What Is the City but the People?* the insistence on location shooting in the *Naked City* reflected the filmmaker's intent to reveal the realities of New York street life to the film viewer.

human interaction, the city is ordered through common cinematic conventions.

Culminating the ninety-second introductory montage, we are shown a scene of one derelict homeless man pinning another in the middle of a filthy city street. The first homeless man lifts his arm, grabs an empty liquor bottle, and delivers a blow to the head of the second—breaking the bottle across his skull. The film cuts to a face shot of the assailant—dazed, vaguely satisfied—then cuts to the figure of his victim flailing below. Freezing the frame, the camera quickly zooms to the bleeding head of the victim. The audio is a frenetic repetition of three piano keys. The film then cuts through a series of dozens of still images of New Yorkers in typical urban settings, holding each frame for no more than a fraction of a second. This continues for nearly twenty seconds. At the end of the sequence, the title of the film appears in rotated red letters affront a multiply-exposed still that seems to indicate the condensed after-image of the preceding visual flow. The scene is an intense assault to the senses. It challenges the limits of the medium's legibility and the viewer's visual cognition (figs. 65-74).

Like the introductory pages of the *Plan for New York City*, the beginning of *What Is the City but the People?* is visual training in preparation for the remainder of the film. The intention is to de-familiarize scenes of everyday city life, allowing the audience to see the images that follow anew. The manic pace of the introduction likewise tunes the viewer to an elevated level of visual acumen. The remainder of the film is often more normative in structure and aesthetic. Thus, only with a renewed attentiveness conditioned by the introduction would the audience fully internalize the more subtle visual codes to follow.

fig.
50

John Peer Nugent. *What Is the City but the People?* 1969. Frame enlargement.

fig.
51

John Peer Nugent. *What Is the City but the People?* 1969. Frame enlargement.

fig.
52

John Peer Nugent. *What Is the City but the People?* 1969. Frame enlargement.

John Peer Nugent. *What Is the City but the People?* 1969. Frame enlargement.

fig.
53

John Peer Nugent. *What Is the City but the People?* 1969. Frame enlargement.

fig.
54

John Peer Nugent. *What Is the City but the People?* 1969. Frame enlargement.

John Peer Nugent. *What Is the City but the People?* 1969. Frame enlargement.

fig.
55

fig.
56

1

Part

John Peer Nugent. *What Is the City but the People?* 1969. Frame enlargement.

fig.
57

John Peer Nugent. *What Is the City but the People?* 1969. Frame enlargement.

fig.
58

fig.
59

John Peer Nugent. *What Is the City but the People?* 1969. Frame enlargement.

fig.
60

John Peer Nugent. *What Is the City but the People?* 1969. Frame enlargement.

John Peer Nugent. *What Is the City but the People?* 1969. Frame enlargement.

fig.
61

John Peer Nugent. *What Is the City but the People?* 1969. Frame enlargement.

fig.
62

McLain Clutter

fig.
63

John Peer Nugent. *What Is the City but the People?* 1969. Frame enlargement.

fig.
64

John Peer Nugent. *What Is the City but the People?* 1969. Frame enlargement.

John Peer Nugent. *What Is the City but the People?* 1969. Frame enlargement.

John Peer Nugent. *What Is the City but the People?* 1969. Frame enlargement.

John Peer Nugent. *What Is the City but the People?* 1969. Frame enlargement.

John Peer Nugent. *What Is the City but the People?* 1969. Frame enlargement.

1

Part

John Peer Nugent. *What Is the City but the People?* 1969. Frame enlargement.

fig.
69

John Peer Nugent. *What Is the City but the People?* 1969. Frame enlargement.

fig.
70

John Peer Nugent. *What Is the City but the People?* 1969. Frame enlargement.

John Peer Nugent. *What Is the City but the People?* 1969. Frame enlargement.

fig.
71

fig.
72

John Peer Nugent. *What Is the City but the People?* 1969. Frame enlargement.

fig.
73

John Peer Nugent. *What Is the City but the People?* 1969. Frame enlargement.

fig.
74

Following the introduction is another montage of urban settings, accompanied by William Whyte's voice-over narration. Contrasting the violent content of the introduction, here the audience is shown scenes of urban dynamics: crowds traversing streets, infrastructural flows, and the placards of corporate offices indexing the movement of capital.[105] By repeatedly cutting between these three categories, each is expressed as a related flow, an input or output, within a city that is understood as a single complex ecological organization (figs. 75-79). Here, circulation is the engine of the city. Whyte's narration introduces the viewer to the Planning Commission's ideas about the benevolence of urban density and development plans for the "National Center." West Midtown is identified as a prime location for expansion, and the film cuts through a series of shots of that neighborhood, highlighting the residents and activities already within the area.

Soon the viewer is introduced to Mary McCarten, a resident of West Midtown and presumptive ambassador for the neighborhood. The rhetoric of the scenes that follow will present McCarten as an everyday New Yorker—a typified individual through whom the viewer is meant to relate. We watch as McCarten exits her apartment building and descends the stair. Upon reaching street level, the camera begins to follow McCarten, tracing her motion through urban space like a single projectile from the preceding montage sequence of urban dynamics. McCarten visits neighbors on a stoop, mixes with traffic at busy intersections, visits street vendors, and so on. As she walks, her motion articulates the kind of fine-grain social interaction within dense urbanism that the film's creators advocate (figs. 80-83).[106] Whyte's narration and McCarten's own words, both folksy in tone, deliver some commentary on the Planning Commission's intentions in West Midtown. But the real content emanates from the example of McCarten's behavior in urban space. She is being presented as an example citizen to the film's audience.

Near the end of the McCarten scene, the audience is shown one last segment of the West Midtown resident—a tracking shot of McCarten walking along a street. The film then cuts abruptly to planning commission chairman Donald Elliott, shot identically, walking another city street. Thus, the persona of the everyday New Yorker is metonymically transferred to the chairman, and the perspective of the everyday citizen is associated with the policies that the chairman advocates (figs. 84-85).

1

Part

105   The structure of this filmic sequence also recalls the early 20th century "city symphony" films, in which the novel kinesis and activity of the metropolis was captured on film. Exemplary among city symphonies in Walther Ruttmann's *Berlin Symphony of a Metropolis* (1927).

106   McCarten's motion and activity also articulates the kind of street life celebrated in New York by Jane Jacobs only a few years prior to *What Is the City but the People?*. See Jane Jacobs, *The Death and Life of Great American Cities* (New York: Random House, 2002).

John Peer Nugent. *What Is the City but the People?* 1969. Frame enlargement.

Much of the following film tracks Elliott. Here, again, the Planning Commission's commitment to the participatory individual within the vast urban ecology is filmically affirmed, now through the example of Chairman Elliott. The audience follows the chairman as he meets with Jaquelin Robertson and Mayor Lindsay on city streets, as he boards the subway, crosses the Brooklyn Bridge, moves in and out of planning meetings, and so on. The cinematography varies, often shot with a handheld camera, producing a shaking frame that adds to the sense of kinesis. For various brief shots, the camera follows behind Elliott, thus suturing his vision, and subject-position, with that of the film spectator. At times, the camera precedes Elliott.

John Peer Nugent. *What Is the City but the People?* 1969. Frame enlargement.

John Peer Nugent. *What Is the City but the People?* 1969. Frame enlargement.

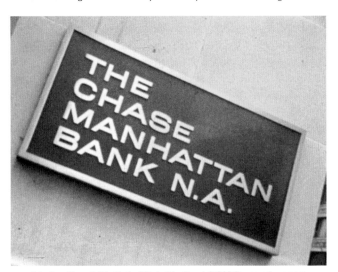

John Peer Nugent. *What Is the City but the People?* 1969. Frame enlargement.

fig.
77

fig.
78

John Peer Nugent. *What Is the City but the People?* 1969. Frame enlargement.

fig.
79

John Peer Nugent. *What Is the City but the People?* 1969. Frame enlargement.

fig.
80

John Peer Nugent. *What Is the City but the People?* 1969. Frame enlargement.

fig.
81

John Peer Nugent. *What Is the City but the People?* 1969. Frame enlargement.

fig.
82

John Peer Nugent. *What Is the City but the People?* 1969. Frame enlargement.

fig.
83

John Peer Nugent. *What Is the City but the People?* 1969. Frame enlargement.

fig.
84

John Peer Nugent. *What Is the City but the People?* 1969. Frame enlargement.

fig.
85

The audience watches Elliott moving forward, the surrounding city and citizens receding behind with each step. Still elsewhere, Elliott walks into the frame from afar, his pace and tempo just divergent enough from those around him to momentarily distinguish himself before moving out of frame. The filmic code approaches didacticism in its delivery of the Planning Commission's ideals. The cumulative message is one of an idealized urban subject who is at once distinct and participatory in the surrounding dynamic urban ecology (fig. 86). The cutting together of the scenes weaves an intricate choreography wherein Elliott repeatedly emerges as an individual from his surroundings before submerging back into the urban flow.

fig.
86

John Peer Nugent. *What Is the City but the People?* 1969. Frame enlargement.

Other scenes of unique significance depict Elliott's motion in tracking shots from an oblique angle, strongly objectified as an individual on the street. In these, the appearance of the physical city is critical to understanding the film's rhetoric. By tracking his motion, the
camera depicts Elliott as effectively static. The city and surrounding
citizens move by as a kinetic background. Here, the city is conceived
as a kind of motion picture against which the urban subject is defined.
Consistent with this assertion is a scene that begins with the planning commission assembled around a conference table discussing
policy. One commissioner is heard advocating new zoning for a
certain deep-Brooklyn neighborhood. The commissioner holds up a
photograph of the streetscape of the neighborhood in question—a
street of almost suburban tranquility. The camera zooms in on the
photograph in the commissioner's hand and then cuts to a scene with
Donald Elliott and the commissioner walking the street depicted. As
the two walk, the commissioner continues to advocate a set of policies for the neighborhood. Elliott is her pensive audience. The camera slowly pans along the houses that compose the streetscape,
registering their positive attributes on film to the soundtrack of the
commissioner's voice-over descriptions (figs. 87-88).

   In this scene, the commissioner's photograph of the pictur-
esque streetscape is held up as irrefutable evidence of the neighborhood's positive qualities. When the camera zooms in on the photograph and then cuts to a scene within the depicted street, now occupied
by the commissioner and Donald Elliott, the film rhetorically posits
the streetscape as an occupiable image. The panning camera, assessing the charms of the houses in the neighborhood, duplicates and
elaborates the evidence offered by the commissioner's snapshot. The

fig.
87

John Peer Nugent. *What Is the City but the People?* 1969. Frame enlargement.

fig.
88

John Peer Nugent. *What Is the City but the People?* 1969. Frame enlargement.

analytic vision of Chairman Elliott is associated with the pan of the camera across the streetscape—substituting the cinematic image for the vision of the individual walking the city street.

Prevalent throughout *What Is The City But the People?* are often unsettling images of urban violence and blight. As in the events described in the introductory montage, such scenes are often presented in highly aestheticized and sophisticated cinematic rhetoric. One example is a scene set in central Brooklyn. A segment of Flatbush Avenue is documented in a remarkably attenuated one-minute tracking shot. The scene portrays blocks of leveled or crumbling buildings, empty urban lots fenced with razor wire and abandoned storefronts. Near the end of the shot, the camera tracks past a child standing alone in middle distance of a vast empty lot. The child appears subsumed, eerily afloat in the surrounding emptiness (figs. 89-91). The velocity of the tracking shot, at the rate of a car moving along the road, stands in stark contrast to the rubbled stasis of the neighborhood depicted—and doubly so for the lone child whose unwavering motionlessness is absolute. Here, the cinematic technique makes the derelict space of the city highly affective. The neighborhood and child alike appear to belong to a different temporality. They are literally and rhetorically left behind in a time-space that diverges from that of the tracking camera, and thus the subject positions of the audience. The filmic code begs an emotive response from the audience, and by extension, from the city's citizens. Adding to the audience's engagement is a strange beauty in the depicted blight. The crumbling buildings resemble a finely patinaed model. The vast vacant lots evince a sublime spatiality. The piles of rubble and boarded storefronts throughout register on the celluloid as a richly textural composition.

John Peer Nugent. *What Is the City but the People?* 1969. Frame enlargement.

fig.
89

John Peer Nugent. *What Is the City but the People?* 1969. Frame enlargement.

fig.
90

A similar scene depicts Soleval Martinez, a former resident of a south Bronx slum whose family had recently been moved to an apartment building that was renovated through a city program. Martinez and the film crew visit his old apartment, which had then been squatted by drug addicts. As Martinez narrates his life, the camera pans across the apartment revealing littered floors, crumbling plaster, and a bathtub apparently filled with sewage. The viewer is afforded a montage of detail shots of spoons used to liquefy heroin and burnt cigarette butts, spliced between close-ups of Martinez's face (figs. 92-94). The *content* of the images is alarming. But the images themselves have a strange allure. They are vivid, dappled with texture and light; if not conventionally beautiful, disarming in their resolution.

John Peer Nugent. *What Is the City but the People?* 1969. Frame enlargement.

John Peer Nugent. *What Is the City but the People?* 1969. Frame enlargement.

Part 1

John Peer Nugent. *What Is the City but the People?* 1969. Frame enlargement.

fig.
93

John Peer Nugent. *What Is the City but the People?* 1969. Frame enlargement.

fig.
94

One might question why any city would sanction the dissemination of images of such deplorable conditions within its own borders— much less a city becoming newly savvy about the power of its mediated representation. No doubt, this footage was meant to seduce sympathy from a dwindling middle class that had grown suspicious of aid to the poor.[107] These scenes were also likely meant to rally cooperation from the poor themselves by providing information on the ways the city was coming to their aid. In either case, the intensity of the images may have overshot the mark.

Another effect was likely unintended but certainly more profound. These scenes resonate with those in several commercial films shot in New York at the time, revealing the contributions of Arthur Ornitz. The cinematographer's work on *Midnight Cowboy* is exemplary. There, the protagonist is a male prostitute who finds himself in various blighted portions of lower Manhattan. As in *What Is the City But the People?*, scenes shot in these areas simultaneously evince repulsion and attraction—the depraved content commingling with an allure that derives from the aesthetic effect of the cinematography. The blighted city appears *real*, wrapped up in nostalgic sentiments for a later-day urbanism, and seducing desire for authenticity. The narrative accompanying commercial films like *Midnight Cowboy* contributes to these seductions of desire. As the viewer is prompted to identify through the protagonist, the ego-ideal is stimulated, attendant to a yearning to inhabit those spaces inhabited by the protagonist in a vain attempt to satiate desire for the ideal self. Critically, the simultaneous circulation of films like *Midnight Cowboy* and the planning commission's film would have created an intermingling of their audiences. Citizens watching the latter may have brought to the images of urban decay within expectations, desires and attitudes that were prefigured through encounters with the former. Thus, the presumed intentions of the city—to gain the sympathy of the middle class, the cooperation of the poor—would have been complicated by complex webs of subjective affect and association among the audience of *What Is the City But the People?* The media audience and citizens of the city were complexly intertwined; the apparatus grew still more.

Complex, fragmentary, and discursive connections run dendritic between Mayor Lindsay's efforts to draw film and television productions to New York and the policies of his planning commission. Economic opportunities afforded to the film industry by the mayor's policies stocked New York with entertainment industry

---

107 This supposition is based on statements within the pages of the *Plan for New York City*, such as "One of the major discontents of many middle- class neighborhoods is the feeling that blacks and Puerto Ricans are having too much done for them as it is..." Elliott, *Critical Issues*, 5.

personnel. The expertise of these individuals was synergistic with the ideology of a planning commission that was quickly coming to terms with the value of media in inflecting the behaviors of the citizens of New York—a city that seemingly defied conventional planning. Tax revenues from film and television production in New York added gravely needed income to the city's tax base. This income could be allocated to the city's underfunded offices, including the City Planning Commission. Continued media production in New York, aided by a shift toward decentralization in Hollywood and the end of the film production code, popularized the mediated image of New York's urban blight. And by conceiving of New York through various mediatic registers in their policies, the planning commission played upon the expectations of those exposed to the city through its renewed presence in film and television. As the proceeding chapters will show, the Planning Commission's policies would eventually implant mediatic understandings of the city within the material New York to be experienced by the urban subject.

As in the Foucaultian apparatus, the connections between these sets of policy emerged at the interplay between intentions. At a time when the resilience of both New York City and the Hollywood production system were very much in question, rich interconnections between acts and circumstances emanating from both engaged one-another to buttress their mutual endurance. For the Hollywood production system, the apparatus aided in the persistence of its reign as a dominant power of cultural production. In the case of New York City, the apparatus aided in nothing less than assuring the continuity of the solvency of city governance, but all-the-while underwriting a paradigm shift in the nature of urbanity. This shift is familiar—encompassing both the discourse of the city as spectacle discussed in the introduction of this volume and related discussions of neoliberal urbanity. Both articulate the moment when cities begin to trade in economies of their own representations, building as Mumford presciently had it, "shadow worlds" of previous urbanisms. The latter effect can be elaborated by returning to the sense of the apparatus as it has emerged in media theory.

By any reading of the apparatus theory of cinema, when providing economic incentives to the film industry to shoot in New York, Lindsay's policies made the city complicit in the financial aspects of what Christian Metz termed the *cinematic institution*. More profound is the way in which the planning policies crafted during Lindsay's tenure that conceived of the city through various mediatic registers may have exploited systems of desire for the image of New York that the cinematic institution forged within spectators. By using the relationship between the spectator and media as a conceptual abstraction for the relationship between the urban subject and the city, the planning policies drafted during the Lindsay administration would figure a city uniquely designed to provoke desirable ego identifications among urban subjects first introduced to New York through its filmic presence. New York's renaissance in the decades following the media industry's dramatic return to the city—a renaissance fueled largely by an influx of young professionals with renewed *desire* for urban lifestyles—might provide evidence to precisely such a provocation.

Thus the dendritic tangle of economic, affective, and material connections described here, and no doubt more—too many and too complex to assess exhaustively—compose the eponymous apparatus of this book. The apparatus, however indeliberate in emergence, constituted the urban context in which architecture and urban design for New York City would be received in the years following. In such a context, urban representations and urban reality collude and commingle, with the former attaining unprecedented agency and ideological valence. In the chapters that follow, actors, ideas or objects enrolled within the apparatus are traced through their future entanglements in order to more directly analyze the nature of urban space and buildings in this paradigm. For the contemporary designer, the analyses herein should constitute a sort of foreshadowing—a prequel to the elaborate interconnections between media ecologies, economics, and subjectivities that no doubt constitute our contemporary urban contexts.

Part 2

The City

Spectator

In the early 1960s the New York City Planning Commission, under the leadership of Chairman James Felt, took on the long overdue task of revising comprehensive zoning in New York City.[1] The standing law was a 1916 resolution, the first comprehensive zoning document in America, and by most accounts a historic success in balancing public interest and economic vitality. However, by 1960 the document was long overdue for revision. Among its most obvious flaws was a projected building bulk that would have allowed a population of 55 million residents. In 1960, it was clear that such a number was both implausible and untenable. New York had a population of less than 8 million people, and at that, congestion and crowding was among the city's most pressing issues. A population of 55 million residents seemed unthinkable. Nevertheless, the city needed to plan for growth in order to sustain continued economic development. Despite problems with urban congestions, New York had just experienced the first decade-over-decade population *loss* in its history, with more than 100,000 residents leaving the city's borders.[2] White flight to the suburbs was among the culprits. While the dramatic population decline of the coming decades was not yet imminent, the fiscal void left by a fleeing middle class was becoming palpable.[3] New taxable activity was needed, which the commission intended to encourage by allowing the development of office buildings at a high density. Such density would only serve to exacerbate congestion and crowding. Thus, an impasse was reached between the necessity for humane conditions for the individual on the street and the equally pressing necessity for an economically sustainable city.

Felt's commission sought to address this impasse by including the city's first incentive zoning initiative in their 1960 resolution. Inspired by the plaza at Mies van der Rohe's recently completed Seagram Building, the new policy gave FAR (Floor Area Ratio) bonuses to developers for providing plazas at the bases of their office towers.[4] Thus, density could be increased while improving quality of life for the public through the provision of open space, light, and air. By the late 1960s, when the Lindsay Administration took office, most regarded

1   For one account of this period, see Carter Horsley, "The Sixties," in *Planning the Future of New York City: A Conference Celebrating the 40ᵗʰ Anniversary of the New York City Planning Commission* (New York, New York City Planning Commission, 1979), 29.

2   See "Excerpts From Paunch Report to Wagner on Need for New Housing Board," *The New York Times*, March 10, 1960, in which J. Anthony Paunch, Mayor Wagner's special advisor on housing and urban renewal discusses, among other topics, the economic impact of the loss of middle-class population, and the pervasive problem of residential and vehicular congestion.

3   This was due to a loss of income tax and a loss of overall taxable economic activity that the middle class sustained. At the same time, a rise in lower-income resident population, many of whom were minorities, strained the city's expenses. for social services. See "Text of Summary of Report of State Commission on City's Government System," *The New York Times*, February 1, 1960.

4   This incentive zoning initiative was one of 850 zoning changes in the 1960 revision. The plaza bonus allowed developers to add ten square feet of floor area to that typically allowed for every one square foot of plaza space provided. See "City Zoning Gaining Support," *The New York Times*, September 11, 1960.

the city's incentive zoning program as a failure. As famously described in Peter Blake's editorial "Slaughter on Sixth Avenue," the majority of the buildings resulting from the policy were generic to the point of sterility, and the acres of new plazas these structures provided were often lifeless interruptions within Manhattan's urban fabric.[5]

Such was the state of affairs in 1972, when William H. Whyte began his study of the use of New York City plaza spaces resulting from incentive zoning, part of a larger examination called *The Street Life Project*.[6] Whyte brought to the study his experience working with the New York City Planning Commission as a writer for the 1969 *Plan for New York City*, and as narrator of the film version of the document, *What Is the City But the People?*. He was therefore intimately familiar with the ideas running through Lindsay's Planning Commission. As discussed in Part 1, prominent among these ideas was a seemingly contradictory pairing: the simultaneous celebration of the quasi-organic, ecological dynamics of urban density, and a commitment to the agency of the individual as the unit through which such dynamics might be inflected. It is likely that Whyte was instrumental in the promotion of this pair of concepts. Understanding a broader expanse of Whyte's work is helpful in reconstructing his contributions.

William Whyte's emergence as a public intellectual paralleled the publication of his 1956 book, *The Organization Man*. In the book, Whyte decries what he called the *rootlessness* of the mid-century American subject. Whyte argued that such a condition was caused by the fall of a once-dominant system of social organization, the *protestant ethic*.[7] Building on the work of Alexis de Tocqueville and Max Weber, Whyte's particular characterization of the Protestant Ethic described a sense of individualism that helped to drive the rapid development of the United States from its inception to post-war prosperity.[8] Whyte wrote that the protestant ethic held that the "pursuit of individual salvation through hard work, thrift, and competitive struggle is the heart of the American achievement."[9] Not unlike other theories of American exceptionalism through staunch individualism, Whyte claimed that the protestant ethic ultimately purported that what was best for the individual was also best for society, as each individual's drive ultimately contributed to the prosperity of the country as a whole.[10] Writing as if an ethnographer of his own culture, Whyte never directly endorses the Protestant ethic. Rather, he

5   Peter Blake, "Slaughter of Sixth Avenue," *Architectural Forum*, June 1965, 13–19.
6   Whyte, *City: Rediscovering the Center* (New York: Doubleday, 1988), 104.
7   Whyte adapted the term "protestant ethic" from the work of Max Weber, who originated the term in order to describe the role of the Calvinist self-discipline and sense of divine "calling" in the emergence of capitalism and the organization of labor therein. See Max Weber, *The Protestant Ethic and the Spirit of Capitalism* (New York:

Scribner, 1930). Weber first published the book in two parts in the *German Archiv Fur Sozialwissenschaft und Sozialpolitik* in 1904–5.
8   William Whyte, *The Organization Man* (Philadelphia: University of Pennsylvania Press, 1956), 5.
9   Whyte, *The Organization Man*, 4.
10 One example is the novelist Ayn Rand's philosophy of Objectivism, which similarly celebrates individual ambition as the impetus for societal wellbeing. See: Leonard Peikoff, *Objectivism: The Philosophy of Ayn Rand* (1991).

placed importance on the idea as a pervasive mythology that had been instrumental in bringing prosperity to United States and granting a sense of cohesiveness to American culture.

According to Whyte, in mid-century America the Protestant ethic was no longer a dominant and binding mythology. In its place, a new driving social contract had emerged, the *social ethic*. The latter was administered by the swell of large corporations throughout the country, and urged the individual's sublimation into society, or into what Whyte called the *organizational system*. The social ethic held that "Man exists as a unit of society. Of himself, he is isolated, meaningless; only as he collaborates with others does he become worthwhile, for by sublimating himself in the group, he helps produce a whole that is greater than the sum of its parts."[11] In return for the individual's allegiance to the organizational system, one was granted a sense of belonging that answered cultural rootlessness. The subjectivity of this system was Whyte's eponymous Organization Man. In carefully measured words, Whyte cautioned against the corporate administration of society in lieu of the individualism that he saw as foundational of American culture.[12]

Carefully distinguishing the relationships between the individual and the system in the protestant and social ethics, Whyte dwelt on the insistence on group "harmony" in the latter.[13] The social ethic demanded the absolute conformity of its subjects in order to project a harmonious collective. In this top-down organizational model, the contribution of each individual is channeled into one collective goal. The Protestant ethic, in contrast, celebrated individual ambition. More of a bottom-up model, it was through the competitive dynamics between individuals, with each competing for success, that a better society emerged. Hence, within Whyte's theorization of the Protestant ethic one might recognize the foreshadowing of that seemingly contradictory pair of ideas now familiar from Lindsay's Planning Commission. The Commission's celebration of *dense urban dynamics* can be understood as a conceptual parallel to Whyte's description of the *competitive dynamic* between groups of self-interested individuals. The Commission's simultaneous belief in the *agency of the citizen* within dense urbanism parallels Whyte's description of the valorization of the *individual* in the Protestant ethic.[14] In both models, a better whole emerges from the dense and dynamic interaction of distinct parts.

According to Whyte, the Organization Man typically resided within the atomizing patterns of development of American suburbia.

11 Whyte, *The Organization Man*, 7.
12 Whyte, *The Organization Man*, 12–15.
13 Whyte, *The Organization Man*, 8.

14 One might also recognize a conceptual resemblance to the manner of bottoms-up, emergent urbanism advocated by Jane Jacobs. See Jane Jacobs, *The Death and Life of Great American Cities* (New York: Random House, 1992).

In fact, he devoted an entire section of his book to examining the relationships between the suburbs and the social ethic.[15] Critically, the Organization Man left his suburb daily to commute to work in corporate headquarters in urban business centers. Hence, in 1972 when Whyte began his study of the effects of New York City plaza spaces resultant from the city's incentive zoning program—plazas that most often fronted corporate office towers in the city's business centers— the presence of the Organization Man must have loomed large in Whyte's subconscious. As Whyte's investigation took shape, the complex relationships between individuals in urban space was the primary focus of his study. Thus, while the study was intended to gather information for use in the design of more vital plazas, a latent intention may also be identified—an attempt to reconcile a problematic individual-to-collective relationship that came attendant to the presence of the Organization Man. In this case, public space became the medium through which this relationship would be reconciled. An entity often associated with notions of the common, here public, space needed to be calibrated to both constitute an arena for urban collectivity, and to encourage individuation among a subjectivity that habitually sought sublimation.

The methodology Whyte applied to his study of urban plazas is critical to this story, resonating deeply with the relationships between media production and urban planning described in the first part of this book. Whyte relied heavily on filmic observation.[16] By filming the daily use of urban plazas he sought to gauge their successes and failures, and to reveal the complex intersubjective relationships therein (figs. 1-2). The urbanist wrote about his work years later in his book *City: Rediscovering the Center.* Whyte noted:

> We used photography a lot: 35mm for stills, Super 8 for time-lapse, and 16mm for documentary work. With the use of a telephoto lens, one can easily remain unnoticed, but we found that the perspective was unsatisfactory for most street interchanges. We moved in progressively closer until we were five to eight feet from our subjects. With a spirit level atop the camera and a wide-angled lens, we could film away with our backs half turned and thus remain unnoticed—most of the time.[17]

Here, Whyte's description of his observation process is critical. By holding his camera with his "back half turned," Whyte often forfeited

15   Whyte, *The Organization Man,* 267–392.
16   Whyte combined his filmic observation with common methods of sociological research such as interviews. In using film, Whyte was tacitly engaging a discussion on the use of film and photography in research for the social sciences ongoing at the time. For one concise source of the state of this discussion, see Jay Ruby, "Is an Ethnographic Film a Filmic Ethnography?" *Studies in the Anthropology of Visual Communication,* vol. 2, no. 2 (Fall 1975): 105–111.
17   Whyte, *City: Rediscovering the Center* (New York: Doubleday, 1988), 4.

William H. Whyte recording activity in urban space.

fig.
1

direct observation of the city for its filmic registration. As he sought to understand the complex individual-to-whole relationships that emerged in the dynamics of urban plazas, the camera became a clinical tool for extracting these embedded urban organizations. Thus, the phenomena Whyte observed were implicitly cinematic. Treating the city as found, its flows and metabolisms, as a vast second-nature to be studied in the field, Whyte recorded the crossing

fig.
2

William H. Whyte recording activity in urban space.

patterns and syncopations of pedestrian traffic, the varying distribution of stationary plaza occupants, the patterning and clustering of conversations across plazas, and a collection of other organizations that occur in motion and over time.

Today, Whyte's methods may seem unremarkable. With the present ubiquity of all manner of media, it is a truism that we are always conducting urban life under the surveillance of some mediatic device. Even in 1972, the surge of media production entering New York City as a result of Mayor Lindsay's policies may have begun to naturalize the presence of film cameras in urban space, while the swell of documentaries treating urban issues in the preceding decades made the city a common subject of study through media.[18] And yet, it is *because* of these developments that Whyte's methods gain importance. The apparatus described in Part 1 of this book: the emergence of location-shot media production in New York, the conceptual resonance between this activity and the policies of the Planning Commission, the interpersonnel and financial symbiosis between the media industries and the city, all enrich the significance of Whyte's methods. Within such a context, the use of a film camera to observe urban life might have a far more instrumental effect than expected.

Also adding significance to Whyte's methodology was one of the sixteen spaces that he chose to begin his study, the plaza at Mies van der Rohe's Seagram Building.[19] Whyte saw the vital plaza at the Seagram as a rare successful specimen whose attributes had yet to be thoroughly explicated. Using hand-held cameras and mounting 16mm units on the Racquet and Tennis Club across Park Avenue, Whyte sought to register on film the patterns of the Seagram's use by the public (fig. 3). This selection of an exemplar is significant for reasons beyond the space's vitality. With this choice, Whyte tacitly engaged in conceptualizations of the Seagram by critics before and after his study that have identified precisely the kind of mediatic ubiquity that characterizes contemporary urbanism, latent within the Seagram itself.[20]

Focusing the scope of his camera, Whyte nominated the Seagram's plaza as a stage, akin to the set for a television drama embedded

18   See Part 1 of this book for a brief discussion of the swell of documentary work in the late 1950s and early 1960s.

19   The sixteen spaces Whyte observed in his analysis were the plazas at 77 Water Street, the Time Life Building, the Exxon Building, the GM Building, the Seagram Building, the J.C. Penney Building, 345 Park Avenue, the Burlington Building, 227 Park Avenue, 630 5th Avenue, the CBS Building, the Pan Am Building, the ITT Building, Lever House, 280 Park Avenue, as well as Paley Park and Exxon Minipark. Despite the length of this list, the plaza at the Seagram seems to have been central to Whyte's study and thoughts, as it is—by a wide margin—the single most recurrent space discussed in Whyte's recounting of his study.

20   Reinhold Martin, for example, has written about the Seagram that "no single building has served more effectively as a totem for thinking about the relation of architecture and mass media in the context of the North American culture industry than Ludwig Mies van der Rohe's Seagram Building." Reinhold Martin, *The Organizational Complex* (Cambridge: MIT Press, 2003), 6. See also: Reinhold Martin, "Atrocities. Or, Curtain Wall as Mass Medium," *Perspecta*, vol. 32, Resurfacing Modernism (New York: MIT Press, 2001).

fig.
3

The Seagram Building, captured from the roof of the Racquet and Tennis Club. Still from William H. Whyte's *The Social Life of Small Urban Spaces*, 1980.

in the city. With this, he confirmed a strong implication in the language of the building. The symmetrical relationship of the Seagram to the Racquet and Tennis Club—with its anthropomorphic façade gazing back—initiates a dialogue between the Seagram and its surroundings that suggests an audience / stage division (figs. 4-5). This reading is substantiated by the elevation of the Seagram's plaza three steps above the surrounding context, creating a sectional division between city and plaza that parallels the audience / stage condition. The surface of this stage is covered with an abstract grid of pavers. Together, the grid of pavers creates a ground that objectifies those who traverse it, making them *theatrical players* in an urban spectacle for surrounding onlookers. In this way, the plaza assumes a mediatic quality as it absorbs, registers, and re-presents the surrounding urban kinesis.

Whyte seems to have recognized these qualities, as the capacity of the Seagram's plaza to render its occupants *theatrical players* certainly gained his attention. While never using this precise terminology, the roles played by individuals within the plaza were of particular interest to his study. Writing about his analysis years later, Whyte's discussion of the Seagram's plaza colors the space as a kind of a petri dish for culturing urban characters. Whyte playfully labeled those he filmed as the "girl watchers," the "lovers," the "camera bugs," and more.[21] Critically, none of Whyte's many character types are described as genuine identities. They are never *authentic* subjectivities. Rather, Whyte describes the "girl watchers," "camera bugs" and more as roles that are self-consciously played, or assumed. Elaborating on this condition, Whyte wrote:

21   Whyte, *City: Rediscovering the Center*, 107.

Of the men up front the most conspicuous are the girl watchers. As I have noted, they put on such a show of girl watching as if to indicate that their real interest is not so much the girls as the show.[22]

And later:

There is a beauty that is beguiling to watch, and one senses that the *players* are quite aware of themselves. You can see this in the way they arrange themselves on ledges and steps. They often do so with a grace that they must appreciate themselves. With its brown-gray setting, Seagram is the best of *stages*—in the rain too, when an umbrella or two puts spots of color in the right places, like Corot's red dots.[23]

fig.
4

The Seagram Building as screen and stage. Photograph by McLain Clutter.

fig.
5

The Seagram Building as screen and stage. Photograph by McLain Clutter.

22   Whyte, *City: Rediscovering the Center*, 107.   23   Whyte, *City: Rediscovering the Center*, 108. Emphasis added.

Apparent from Whyte's text, he thought of the urban characters he classified as *roles* played by individuals who had become *character actors*. These were parts played by individuals who had somehow internalized the script. Thus as narratives of urban life in New York were being produced by the media industries at increasing volumes, Whyte understood the urban subject to be analogous to a character in a film or television production.

Here, it is constructive to reflect again on the latent presence of Whyte's Organization Man in the plaza at the Seagram. In a passage in *The Organization Man* Whyte describes a subversive tactic through which one may exercise agency within the social ethic. Perhaps counter-intuitively, this required that one self-consciously *play the role* of a typical Organization Man. Whyte explained that when exercising such a tactic the Organization Man's:

> ... surface uniformities can serve quite well as protective coloration. The organizational people who are best able to control their environment rather than be controlled by it are well aware that they are not too easily distinguishable from the others in the outward obeisance paid to the good opinions of others. And that is one of the reasons they do control. They disarm society.[24]

Whyte's unusual text suggests that the Organization Man might assume the outward appearance of a conventional subjective type as a kind of *camouflage*, disguising a deeper level of individualism. Similarly, the urban plaza occupants that Whyte wrote about several years later *posture* self-conscious subjective types, potentially veiling their underlying individual identities. With this, it seems, one method through which the spatiality of the urban plaza might engage the problematic individual-to-collective relationship that is characteristic of the Organization Man is clarified. The plaza provides a stage within which the Organization Man may self-consciously assume a conventional role as camouflage for surreptitious subjective individuation. The successful interaction between such self-conscious players within urban space constitutes one aspect of Whyte's peculiar notion of collectivity. But this story becomes more complex through a further assessment of the mediatic qualities of the Seagram.

According to theorists such as Andre Bazin and Roland Barthes, cinema and photography are indexical, in the semiotic sense of the term.[25] These media create a filmic *registration* of that which is depicted, communicating to their audience by recalling the presence

Chapter 2

Part I

24 Whyte, *The Organization Man*, 11.
25 See, for example, Andre Bazin (trans. Timothy Barnard), *What is Cinema* (Montreal: Caboose, 2009) and Roland Barthes, *Camera Lucida: Reflections on Photography* (New York: Farrar, Straus and Giroux, 1980). Michael Hays has also called the Seagram Building an 'absent-presence,' but in a different sense. See Michael Hays, "Abstraction's Appearance," in *Autonomy and Ideology: Positioning an Avant-Garde in America*, ed. Robert Somol (New York: Monacelli Press, 1997), 278–291.

of their absent subject matter. One's experience of the Seagram may provide similar visual impressions.[26] Viewed from the street, the Seagram, its plaza, and inhabitants commingle in a visual play of reflection, overlay, and screening that makes ambiguous the distinction between absence and presence, object and image. The building's curtain wall reflects the activity in the plaza and the surrounding city back towards the onlooker, creating a great urban screen that overlays a reflected image on one's view of the Seagram and the occupants inside. Hence, the images of occupants and the adjacent city flatten at the mediating membrane of the glass curtain wall. They are apprehended, equally, as an absent-present urban imaginary (fig. 6). The mullion pattern of the curtain wall regulates the flattened image and suggests rhyming relationships with similar adjacent buildings that are reflected—again confusing object for image, absence for presence, and architectural composition for imaginary format. Viewed in relation to the visual complexity of the curtain wall above, the plate-glass lobby enclosure metonymically assumes the character of the curtain wall, also articulating a taught membrane that flattens occupants within into a surface image. And as these lobby occupants move in and out between lobby and plaza, they conflate "character" in the plaza and image-occupant of the Seagram Building.

One may gather a similarly mediatic impression from within the building's plaza. This reading flips the stage / audience division, constituting the plaza's occupants as an audience and the surrounding city as urban spectacle. In this case, the plaza operates as a point of urban erasure understood as a void or gap in the city, temporarily suspending urban continuity. Several theorists of early film have described the spatial condition of the urban cinema, with its comfortable chairs, air-conditioning, and all-encompassing darkness, as promoting a suspension of conscious understanding of one's body in space, in stark contrast to one's presence in their surrounding cities. The plaza at the Seagram can be understood similarly, as its formal separation from the surrounding urban flow provides a space from which to cast a voyeuristic gaze. In this sense, the plaza

---

26   Soon after its construction, a *Time Magazine* critic wrote that the Seagram was an "accent of emptiness," at once highlighting its presence (as accent) and absence (as emptiness). "Monument in Bronze," *Time*, Monday, March 3, 1958, 52–55. Vincent Scully later remarked that the Seagram tower set afloat in its plaza was both "a purely freestanding presence" as well as the "ideal background architecture" by virtue of its serial reproducibility. [Vincent Scully, "The Death of the Street," in *Modern Architecture and Other Essays* (Princeton: Princeton University Press, 2005), 195.] Thus, to Scully, the building was both imminently extant, and receding into the background to the limit-point of absence. K. Michael Hays has undoubtedly contributed the most productive insight for the present discussion along these lines. Calling the Seagram a "handmade readymade," the theorist eloquently noted that the Seagram "is a cutout in the city, a literal nothing endowed nevertheless with a positive presence through its material and dimensional precision." (Hays, 283) In the same essay, Hays later surmises that "in the Seagram project there is only a visual field so homogenous, spread out, and intense that one wants to adopt the painting critic's nomenclature and call it optical. There is a part of the Seagram that addresses itself to the eye alone ..." (Hays, 288). Thus, with Hays, the Seagram's serial reproducibility, dual status of presence, and appeal to a proto-mediatic visual register is mobilized in one essay.

fig.
6

Reflections on the Seagram's curtain wall. Photograph by McLain Clutter.

Chapter I

2

Part

becomes a spatial interface for the reproduction of a state of anonymous vision characteristic of many media.[27]

Again, these are qualities of the Seagram that Whyte seems to have observed, as a large part of his plaza study was spent assessing precisely the requirements for maintaining this spatial character. His solutions revolve primarily around the calibration of a single, unlikely, urban amenity: seating. For Whyte, seating was the necessary complement to dense dynamics in urban plazas.[28] The flow of theatrical character types was visible only when adequate spaces of repose were supplied from which to view the unfolding drama. Such spaces of repose become points of bodily removal, or suspension, which enable plaza occupants to figure the urban context as a dynamic urban imaginary. While Whyte never offers precisely this analysis, it is consistent with his description of the experience of viewing the dynamics of the plaza at the Seagram—a description that is thoroughly aesthetically cinematic:

27   Anonymity among film spectators is a common theme in film theories by a range of thinkers from disparate intellectual traditions. These theories usually describe the experience of the cinema as one in which the individual, engulfed by the darkness of the theatre, is allowed to forget his/her bodily presence and engage the images on screen in voyeuristic anonymity. For example, philosopher Stanley Cavell has claimed that anonymity among cinema viewers is a natural *extension* of general conditions that exist within the cultural context of the modern world. Cavell wrote: "How do movies reproduce the world magically? Not by literally presenting us with the world, but by permitting us to view it unseen. In viewing films, the sense of invisibility is an expression of modern privacy and anonymity." [Stanley Cavell, *The World Viewed: Reflections on the Ontology of Film* (Cambridge: Harvard University Press, 1979), 75.] Thus, the act of viewing films in a darkened theatre where the spectator may remain *unseen* is an expression of cultural anonymity at large. For Cavell, the success of cinema, then, is based on its

compatibility with general cultural conditions. Cinema answers a societal demand for anonymous viewing, but the cause of that demand is exterior to the subject—within societal conditions of modernity that produce anonymity. Siegfried Kracauer linked spectatorial anonymity to desire for viewing film anonymously (Kracauer, 159–160). Kracauer wrote: "They (*film spectators, subjects*) are not prompted by a *desire* to look at a specific film or to be pleasantly entertained; what they really crave is for once to be *released from the grip of consciousness, lose their identity in the dark*, and let sink in, with their senses ready to absorb them, the images as they happen to follow each other on the screen." (Emphasis added.) For Kracauer, movie attendance creates a pleasing sensation of loss-of-self in which the spectator may view the imaginary on-screen while remaining veiled in darkness—while remaining him/herself unseen. Thus for Kracauer, the success of cinema, while related to larger cultural conditions of modernity, exists at the level of spectatorial craving for anonymous viewing.

Down at eye level the scene comes alive with movement and color—people walking quickly, walking slowly, skipping up steps, weaving in and out on crossing patterns, accelerating and retarding to match the moves of others. Even if the paving and walls are gray, there will be vivid splashes of color—in winter especially, thanks to women's fondness for red coats and colored umbrellas.[29]

This experience is the vision of a stationary urban subject—viewing the surrounding urban scenography while excised from its dynamic flow. The description imbues the plaza occupant with the characteristics of the camera. The occupant is a stationary vision machine, set apart and unnoticed by the surrounding urbanites. The description similarly imparts to the plaza occupant the characteristics of the spectator in the cinema—anonymous and subsumed in space, and intensely engaged in the visual experience of his or her surroundings (fig. 7).

It has been theorized that in cinema the absence-presence of that which is depicted invites spectatorial voyeurism. The spectator's ability to view absent individuals on-screen anonymously, without fear of having his or her gaze returned—without fear of being looked *at*—enables a primary subjective identification with one's vision, as opposed to one's visibility.[30] Within such a condition, a spectator may safely succumb to the pleasures of voyeuristic *desire*. Through Whyte's descriptions of his analyses, it is clear that he valued spatial qualities that provoked a similar visual experience from urban plaza occupants. Whyte even discussed the necessity of maintaining anonymity among plaza occupants, writing:

What makes people uncomfortable is direct eye contact with strangers. True, people like to look at other people, but they don't like to be caught at it, and they don't like to be looked at.[31]

In apparatus theories of cinema, the desire for anonymous viewing is rooted neither simply in larger cultural conditions, nor on the level of the individual. Rather, spectatorial desire is a product of the tautology between the film industry and the spectator within the cinematic institution. More than a subjective affect or an expression of cultural conditions, the desire for anonymous viewing is both the currency that fuels the cinematic institution and one of the products of the institution. Thus, this desire has its roots in both the financial systems of film production, and well as the psychic currencies of the spectators. Most importantly, for the spectators, viewing in anonymity is a mode of subjective *definition* within the cinema. Having suspended their bodily presence amid the comfort and darkness of the theatre, the spectator's primary identification—their primary means of structuring a sense of self—is through their own vision. For Christian Metz, this stems from a treatment of the Lacanian mirror stage. While primary identification in the mirror stage is with one's reflection, Metz explains that a secondary identification is with one's own vision. This secondary identification becomes the primary means of understanding the self in the cinema. Metz wrote: "The mirror is the site of primary identification. Identification with one's own look is secondary with respect to the mirror, i.e., for a general theory of adult activities, but it is the foundation of the cinema and hence primary when the latter is under discussion: it is *primary cinematic identification...* (Metz's emphasis)." [Christian Metz, *The Imaginary Signifier* (Indianapolis: Indiana University Press, 1977), 56.] Individuation, then, comes by way of a state of anonymous viewing in an environment where an understanding of one's physical placement in space is obscured—replaced with an understanding of self as a seeing mechanism.

28   Whyte, *City: Rediscovering the Center*, 116.
29   Whyte, *City: Rediscovering the Center*, 108.
30   Metz, 35–55.
31   Whyte, *City: Rediscovering the Center*, 111.

No doubt, these ideas entered Whyte's study as an effect of his methodology. By so heavily relying on filmic observation, thus ensuring that his observations were implicitly mediatic, the subject-positions his analyses suggest elide with those of the media spectator. Here, then, a second mode of individuation emerges for the Organization Man populating the plaza at the Seagram. Entering the plaza as a serial type that conforms to the demands of the social ethic, or as an individual who self-consciously plays the role of a character type, he occupies the plaza as anonymous spectator engaging his surroundings as a proto-mediatic imaginary. Such an elision of the subject-position of the urban plaza occupant and the media spectator would only become increasingly habitual as the coming onslaught of media productions that were location-shot in New York intermingled with one's expectation of the directly experienced city.

Adding to this effect is the proliferation of urban plazas created under revisions to New York City's incentive zoning program that resulted from Whyte's study. Released in 1975, the revisions included several sections that seem colored by the ideological residue of Whyte's analytic methods. Among them was a stipulation that 75 percent of the area in new plazas must be visible at all times from the vantage of any plaza occupant—setting the stage for an intricate spatial dialectic of spectacle and spectator across future urban plazas. Another new provision regulated plaza paving patterns, ensuring that the pavement would both complement the sidewalk and announce its exclusion from its surroundings, thus ensuring that the plaza might announce a point of removal from the surrounding city from which to look out. Yet another regulation stated that 50 percent of the ground-level frontage on buildings in plazas must be

fig.
7

Anonymous viewing on the Seagram Building's plaza.
Still from William H. Whyte's *The Social Life of Small Urban Spaces*, 1980.

occupied by retail and galleries. These are programs that presumably require an abundance of the mediating vision glass present at the Seagram.

But perhaps the most telling provision in the revised zoning borrows Whyte's curious obsession with plaza seating. A substantial section stipulated precise amounts, dimensions, and orientations for benches, chairs, and sittable ledges.[32] As explained by Whyte, these seating specifications were carefully calculated to balance one's apprehension of visual density with the necessity to maintain a minimum circumference of personal space around each seated plaza occupant.[33] Each individual could excise him or herself in repose, viewing the surrounding urban spectacle without being physically touched or crowded in a way that would awaken bodily understanding of self-in-space. Thus, as popular culture continues to be saturated with mediated representations of New York that often precede one's direct experience of the city, and all manner of media continue to intertwine and mesh with urban life, there are plazas nested within New York's gridiron whose formal and spatial characteristics have been tailored to seduce the *desires* of a public whose behaviors have been trained through media exposure. Such desire will be discussed further in the chapter that follows.

32   New York City Planning Commission, *New Life for Plazas* (New York, 1975).

33   Whyte, *City: Rediscovering the Center*, 114–128.

Desire

On September 21, 1961, WCBS television station in New York City aired the half-hour documentary *Our Vanishing Legacy* (fig. 8).[34] The film was produced by Gordon Hyatt, who would go on to co-direct *What Is the City but the People?*, and was narrated by Ned Calmer, a veteran WCBS newsman. A product of the station's Public Affairs Department, *Our Vanishing Legacy* sought to inform viewers of the mounting threat to New York City's historic structures, many of which were in danger of demolition to make way for new construction fueling new economic development. Early in the documentary, Calmer leadingly queries his audience: "Are we just tearing down buildings or are we also destroying some of the most precious things in our cultural heritage?" (fig. 9) The question is revealed to be rhetorical, as the newsman further urges viewers to take stock of "the priceless quality of tradition" forever lost with the destruction of so many of the city's landmarks. Effuse with nostalgic sentiments for a city grounded in rich historicity, *Our Vanishing Legacy* implores its audience to reevaluate the stakes of their loss with the demolition of the city's historic structures.

By 1961, the recurrent destruction of New York's aging urban fabric to make room for new development was a well-established practice. Historian Max Page, building upon the reflections of Henry James, has noted that "New York is, always has been, and always will be . . . a 'provisional city,' defined by a 'dreadful chill of change.'"[35] Similar observations of the city's rapid building, demolition, and rebuilding have been credited to critics throughout New York's history.[36] Across this time, advocates for preservation have emerged. Page has vividly detailed the history of the preservationist sentiment in New York in the late 19th and early 20th centuries, a movement allied to goals varying from the veneration of Revolutionary War heroes through the preservation of their former houses, to claims that historic structures could be didactic aids in service of progressive social reform.[37] Such early attempts at asserting historic preservation practices were largely silenced by the 1930s.[38]

By the early 1960s, historic preservation was again emerging as a contemporary issue.[39] As the first documentary advocating the movement in New York, *Our Vanishing Legacy* was an important

34   Jack Gould, "TV: Focus on New York, 3 Shows Take Up Civic Problems, Saving of Old Buildings and Subsurface Facets," *The New York Times*, September 22, 1961.

35   Max Page, *The Creative Destruction of Manhattan, 1900-1940* (Chicago: University of Chicago Press, 1999), 1.

36   Several such sentiments are enumerated by Barbaralee Diamonstein in her book *The Landmarks of New York III*, including quotations from Mayor Philip Hone, Walt Whitman, and others. See

Barabalee Diamonstein, *The Landmarks of New York III* (Harry N. Abrams, Inc. Publishers: New York, 1998), 7–8.

37   Page, 111–143.

38   Page, 142.

39   For one example of the emergent sentiment towards the value of historic preservation, see Ada Louise Huxtable, "Must Urban Renewal Be Urban Devastation?" *The New York Times*, December 24, 1961.

fig.
8

Gordon Hyatt. *Our Vanishing Legacy*, 1961. Frame enlargement.

fig.
9

Gordon Hyatt. *Our Vanishing Legacy*, 1961. Frame enlargement.

contribution to this reemergence. The documentary is a review of some of New York's most threatened historic buildings from the time: Carnegie Hall, Jefferson Market Courthouse, the Broadway Central Hotel, Louis Sullivan's Bayard-Condict Building, and other buildings that either featured unique architectural qualities, or hosted important historic events. In the past, historic preservation had been a cause for the cultural and intellectual elite.[40] By broadcasting *Our Vanishing Legacy* on WCBS, its message could be popularized and communicated to a broader audience than ever before through the most populist of mediums at the time, television.

40   Max Page's account of the diverse agendas of historic movements advocating preservation, and the various intellectual and ideological associations of these movements, makes this point well. Page, 111–143.

Prominent in the documentary are scenes shot at McKim, Mead and White's Pennsylvania Station. Famously, the Station has since been demolished. In its place sits the current Madison Square Garden. *Our Vanishing Legacy* offers rare glimpses of the structure in the months immediately preceding its demolition.[41] It is in these scenes that the film is perhaps most effective. Seducing the viewer with an eclectic array of historical and heroic allusions, *Our Vanishing Legacy* attempts to portray Pennsylvania Station as an indispensable contribution to an urban environment of profound authenticity.

Introducing the segment on the station, Calmer explains that the principal designer of the project was Charles Follen McKim, partner in the practice of McKim, Mead and White. While standing in front of the ghostly presence of McKim's visage, Calmer notes that the architect "could never quite get over the ruins of Imperial Rome, and before he finished his career, he raised up buildings that rivaled the Ceasars" (fig. 10). With this, a claim to the historicity of Pennsylvania Station that repeats throughout the segment is established. While only erected in 1910, Calmer's words suggest that the station instantiates a deep tradition building upon thousands of years of western culture. As such, the building's presence in New York City anchored urban life within a legacy that was enduring and somehow foundational.

Calmer's claims are then echoed through the following footage. From the exterior, the station is pictured in a way that amplifies its monumental presence. While Calmer explains that the structure

II

Chapter

2

Part

fig.
10

Gordon Hyatt. *Our Vanishing Legacy*, 1961. Frame enlargement.

41   Pennsylvania Station was also famously captured in Stanley Kubrick's 1955 film noir, *Killer's Kiss*. For a discussion of the characterizations of post-war urban space distilled in this film, and the depiction of Pennsylvania Station therein, see Edward Dimendberg, *Film Noir and the Spaces of Modernity* (Cambridge: Harvard University Press, 2004), 136–148.

is composed of half a mile of exterior walls, the building is shown in dramatic perspectives that allow it to span the entire frame, or to vanish into seemingly infinite perspectival space (figs. 11-12). In these shots, Pennsylvania Station plays the role of backdrop to the surrounding urban life. Cars and pedestrians move by: temporal, kinetic and fleeting. Meanwhile, the station is their silent witness: static, durational, and timeless. This message is elaborated in the following shots. Pointed upward, the camera captures details of the classical features of the building. Column capitals and coffered ceilings appear in high-contrast chiaroscuro, the effect of an absent Mediterranean sun (figs. 13-14). These details are shown decontextualized and without indication of the surrounding city. Seemingly, they are timeless fragments that might as likely adorn a classical ruin as a train station in New York City. A following shot of the main entrance, which Calmer informs the viewer is larger than the Brandenburg Gate in Berlin, anchors the previous details in their urban context by including the street level (fig. 15). But the tension between the two types of shots remains. The building is portrayed as both timeless and demonstrative of architectural principals that transcend place, and monumentally established in the surrounding city as a visitation of that transcendent legacy.

The trope of cutting between shots of "timeless" classical details and activity on the pedestrian level continues as the documentary treats the building's interior (fig. 16). There, the shots at the pedestrian level exhibit a brisk choreography. Swarms of people are pictured moving through the station's monumental spaces, up and down stairs and escalators (figs. 17-18). Thus, the building assumes a complex temporality. The decontextualized details evince a sense of timelessness in stylistic reference, while the shots at the pedestrian level suggest that the structure is indexical of so many years of New York's passage through time and space. Accompanying and complicating this temporal complexity, the narration recalls Charles Follen McKim's visits to the Baths of Caracalla in Rome, and notes that the travertine used in the station was imported from quarries in the Roman Campagna near Tivoli, where stone was mined to build the Coliseum. Later, a shot of the main concourse is accompanied by narration that informs that the space is larger than the nave of St. Peter's Basilica. Filmed from an elevated vantage, the pedestrians moving through the concourse appear dwarfed. The space seems literally and metaphorically larger than life (fig. 19). Thus, those inside enroll themselves in something profound beyond the register of the single citizen, something that transcends individual experience.

Finally, the documentary visits the train room. There, the glass roof enclosure is shot from below, filtering light through the steel structure to Piranesian effect (figs. 20-21). With that, allusions

fig.
11

Gordon Hyatt. *Our Vanishing Legacy*, 1961. Frame enlargement.

fig.
12

Gordon Hyatt. *Our Vanishing Legacy*, 1961. Frame enlargement.

Gordon Hyatt. *Our Vanishing Legacy*, 1961. Frame enlargement.

fig.
13

Gordon Hyatt. *Our Vanishing Legacy*, 1961. Frame enlargement.

fig.
14

fig.
15

Gordon Hyatt. *Our Vanishing Legacy*, 1961. Frame enlargement.

fig.
16

Gordon Hyatt. *Our Vanishing Legacy*, 1961. Frame enlargement.

Gordon Hyatt. *Our Vanishing Legacy*, 1961. Frame enlargement.

fig.
17

Gordon Hyatt. *Our Vanishing Legacy*, 1961. Frame enlargement.

fig.
18

Gordon Hyatt. *Our Vanishing Legacy*, 1961. Frame enlargement.

fig.
19

again to ancient Rome. Meanwhile, the narration suggests that within the train room "one can sense once again the imperial majesty of the 19th century American railroad." Thus, added and allied to allusions of Roman lineage is a suggestion that the building condenses some essentially American experience.

In sum, the treatment of Pennsylvania Station in *Our Vanishing Legacy* offers its audience complex and combinatory enticements. The narration and images attempt to encompass the building in a deep historical teleology, rooted thousands of years prior. The station is portrayed as exemplary of both a broadly cast notion of western culture and as an effect of fundamentally American cultural traditions. The structure is depicted as simultaneously timeless and transcendent, and monumentally rooted in its surrounding city.

fig.
20

Gordon Hyatt. *Our Vanishing Legacy*, 1961. Frame enlargement.

Gordon Hyatt. *Our Vanishing Legacy*, 1961. Frame enlargement.

fig.
21

Indeed, the documentary offers the viewer an array of visual and rhetorical seductions.

Such seductions did not escape the press at the time. Following its debut, journalists from *The New York Times*, *The New York
Herald Tribune*, *The Daily News*, and *Variety* all lauded *Our Vanishing Legacy*.[42] The *Times* columnist Jack Gould wrote that the film
was "a persuasive plea for preservation of buildings that are a part of
the city's architectural heritage." He followed that the "WCBS is
to be applauded for putting the weight of its editorial force behind
a campaign to save New York from architectural mayhem."[43] Gould's
words, and indeed the documentary itself, exemplify the emergent
cultural sentiment towards the value of historic preservation.

During the building boom of the 1950s, broad portions of
New York were demolished and rebuilt in the form of corporate
modernist towers. To many, the resultant buildings appeared ster-
ile, generic, and lacking some ill-defined quality of humanity that
was gaining cultural currency.[44] As a result, a broadening contin-
gent of the public was beginning to understand New York's historic
structures as tangible indexes of the city's past. Increasingly, such

42   Jack Gould, "TV: Focus on New York, 3 Shows
      Take Up Civic Problems, Saving of Old Buildings
      and Subsurface Facets," *The New York Times*,
      September 22, 1961; "TV in Review," *New York
      Herald Tribune*, September 22, 1961; Ben Gross,
      "TV Considers Our Town; Kovacs as Zany as Ev-
      er," *Daily News*, September 22, 1961; "Our Vanish-
      ing Legacy," *Variety*, September 27, 1961.

43   Jack Gould, "TV: Focus on New York, 3 Shows
      Take Up Civic Problems, Saving of Old Buildings
      and Subsurface Facets," *The New York Times*,
      September 22, 1961.

44   In just one expression of this attitude, in 1963 ar-
      chitecture critic Ada Lousie Huxtable comment-

ed that the newly constructed New York Hilton
at Rockefeller Center had a "glossily impersonal
façade." In the same article, the critic noted that
the new Pan Am Building, then under construction,
was being built using "minimum good materials of
minimum acceptable quality executed with a minimum of imagination." See Ada Louise Huxtable,
"Architecture Stumbles On, Recent Buildings
Are Nothing Much to Brag About," *The New York
Times*, April 14, 1963. Another example is Peter
Blake's 1969 declaration that the then-new buildings on 6th Avenue composed an "antiseptic slab
city." Peter Blake, "Slaughter of Sixth Avenue,"
Architectural Forum, June 1965, 13–19.

material records solicited desire to access the past to which they held witness, for a built environment anchored in historicity, providing *authenticity* to urban life.[45] It was this emergent desire for urban authenticity that *Our Vanishing Legacy* so adeptly leveraged. Such desire would soon find an agent in the city's policies regarding its historic urban fabric.

Preservation Policy

The most commonly sited catalyst for institutionalized landmarks preservation in New York is the 1963 destruction of McKim Mead and White's Pennsylvania Station, the very structure so prominently featured in Hyatt's film.[46] Following this, an alliance of organizations including the Municipal Arts Society, the New York Community Trust, the Action Group for Better Architecture, and the Brooklyn Heights Association persuaded the city to protect its historic structures through the establishment of the Landmarks Preservation Commission in 1965. With the creation of the Commission, twenty original sites were named for preservation, and evolving criteria were instituted to preserve select historic structures and districts in New York City.

When John Lindsay took office one year later, his administration assumed responsibility for the continued application and elaboration of the Landmarks Law. During Lindsay's tenure, important revisions were established, such as a stipulation granting developers the right to sell unused allowable floor area on the site of a landmark building. This revision was meant to discourage litigious action by developers, and to balance the economic necessities of continued urban development with the principle of landmarks preservation. Also during Lindsay's tenure, the mayor's Urban Design Group began a practice of establishing "special zoning districts" in order to tailor development laws to the specificities of areas within the city deemed unique. Many of these special districts were intended to preserve the character of historic streetscapes within the city. Early examples to this effect include a zoning provision to protect the limestone façades of Fifth Avenue from 1971, and a similar provision for Madison Avenue in 1973.

Among the areas that the Urban Design Group protected through special district zoning were neighborhoods that had previously been regarded as blighted and lacking many qualities worthy of preservation. The theatre district around Times Square, then a haven for pornography and street crime, was among the first areas along these lines to receive protection through a special district

45   Interest in historic preservation could also be understood in context to the emergence of postmodern architecture and its renewed valuation of history, tradition, and condemnation of tabula-rasa urban strategies that were institutionalized in the American context in the form of urban renewal.

46   Diamonstein, 8. See also: Nathan Silver, *Lost New York* (New York: Shocken Books), xii.

zoning resolution in 1967. Following this model, other apparently blighted areas such as the South Street Seaport in 1972, and Little Italy and Tribeca in 1976, were protected by special district documents authored by Urban Design Group. An earlier paradigm of planning would have likely recommended these areas for partial demolition and urban renewal. The aging urban fabric might have been understood as supportive of the surrounding crime and vice. Redevelopment strategies would have introduced light, air, and open space in place of cavernous lower Manhattan streets and crammed tenement quarters. What signaled such a paradigm change?

Many contributions might be identified. Certainly, the burgeoning cultural sentiment towards the value of historic preservation was instrumental in the reevaluation of these decaying neighborhoods. The same desire for authenticity awakened by the demolition of Pennsylvania Station was latent in the Planning Commission's special zoning district policies. Also influential must have been the recent battle between Jane Jacobs and Robert Moses over plans for the Cross-Manhattan Expressway. Famously, Jacobs valorized the social dynamics of historic New York City neighborhoods, and her efforts came to exemplify the social unrest often unleashed through top-down planning policies.[47] Certainly, too, by the time some of the special districts were established, the real-estate industry had come to recognize that preservation could be in its best interest, as a cultural reevaluation of historic urban fabric made previously undesirable neighborhoods saleable and tourist-friendly.[48] Indeed, no single driving impetus can be identified for the Planning Commission's ideological change. Rather, the Commission's actions seem motivated by a series of inter-related influences. Among these influences must be included an unlikely factor, Mayor Lindsay's 1966 Executive Order 10. The policy enabling a renewed onslaught of film and television production in the city radically enhanced desire for the city's historic and decaying neighborhoods.

Media and Desire

By its very nature, film solicits audience desire. Christian Metz, an adherent to the apparatus theory of cinema from which this book borrows its name, theorized desire for cinema as a critical participant in the complex exchanges between audience and industry that compose the cinematic institution. According to Metz, audience

47   Jane Jacobs, *The Death and Life of Great American Cities* (New York: Modern Library, 1969), 55–73.
48   Christine Boyer, among others, has argued convincingly that by the 1970s historic preservation was often a tool for neoliberal urban development, preserving and re-staging the visuality of our cities largely in the interest of capital and power. Such a phenomena is part of the larger systematic processes of deindustrialization, theming, and trading in urban image that is characteristic of neoliberal urbanism, and is accepted as an antecedent to this discussion. Christine Boyer, *The City of Collective Memory: Its Historical Imagery and Architectural Entertainment* (Cambridge: MIT Press, 1994), 51–65.

desire is a financial necessity for the film industry, and as the proliferation of mainstream films tutors the audience in modes of spectatorship, the audience collectively tailors the film industry's production as a function of libidinal drive.[49] Metz's formulation of audience desire draws deeply on his reading of Lacan.[50]

In Lacanian theory, subjectivity can be understood as an economy between three levels of identification—the symbolic, the imaginary, and the real. The symbolic describes the world of language wherein a subject understands him or herself as a participant within a continuous network of signifiers and signifieds. The imaginary stage of subjective development precedes the symbolic, and refers to the identification of self-as-image and the formation of the ego-ideal. Metz's film theory addresses the interrelation between these two categories, with an emphasis on the ways in which cinema draws upon the imaginary stage of subjective development. The real, which precedes both the symbolic and the imaginary, comprises the most fundamental levels of subjective formation that resist linguistic or imagistic codification.

According to Metz, as an *imaginary* medium, cinema recalls the Lacanian mirror-stage, the event in an infant's life in which he or she first recognizes his or her reflection in a mirror and therefore understands self-as-other or self-as-image.[51] The composed image returns to the infant a cohesive understanding of self that exceeds the comparatively rudimentary developmental state of the child. Thus, the self-image is instrumental in the formation of the ego-ideal, or the ideal self. Throughout life, the subject's inability to become the ideal image of self is the source for insatiable desire.[52] Metz's film theory relies on his own corollary to the mirror stage, wherein an infant stands affront a mirror with his or her mother. In this scenario the infant is challenged to identify the self-as-image, the other, and the *other-as-image*. Metz argued that in this complex associative moment the mother is metonymically associated with the infant, and then the infant identifies through the image of the other (the mother) on a secondary level, as a kind of extension of the identification with the ego-ideal.[53] Metz therefore argues that cinema, which is always presenting the other-as-image, is always coupled with solicitations of desire first forged in the mirror stage.

Metz further contended that cinema also effects desire through another Lacanian concept, the scopic drive, the desire to

Chapter II

Part 2

49 Christian Metz, *The Imaginary Signifier* (Indianapolis: Indiana University Press, 1977), 42–57.

50 The application of Lacan by apparatus theorists of cinema has not been unanimously endorsed. For one critique of the common use of Lacanian thought in apparatus theory, see Richard Allen, *Projecting Illusion: Film Spectatorship and the Impression of Reality* (Cambridge: Cambridge University Press, 1995), 7–39.

51 Ibid.

52 Jacques Lacan, "The Mirror Stage as Formative of the I Function as Revealed in Psychoanalytic Experience," in *Ecrits*, trans. Bruce Fink (New York: W.W. Norton & Company, 2006), 75–81.

53 Metz, 45–46.

see, or voyeuristic desire. In Metz's description, the scopic drive in-
augurates a tortured pursuit, as the physical distance required to *see*
ensures that the object of desire is never obtained. Thus, the scopic
drive is constantly titillated, never satiated. Within cinema, such tit-
illation is complexly inscribed and redoubled. The viewer's scopophilic impulse to obtain the figures depicted, or to occupy the spaces viewed is hopelessly unattainable by virtue of the absence-presence
of the cinematic signifier.[54] While the objects, spaces and characters
depicted are vividly present as visual effect, they are nevertheless
fundamentally absent and unattainable for the viewing subject.

What might these theories reveal about audience desire for the
city as depicted in media enabled by Mayor Lindsay's Executive
Order 10? As recounted in the first part of this book, with Executive
Order 10, Mayor Lindsay granted unprecedented incentives to the
media industries to draw major location-shot film and television productions to New York. The order coincided with the Motion Picture
Association of America's repeal of the Production Code, which enforced moral standards in Hollywood films.[55] As a result of this conjuncture, many of the films produced in New York in the late 1960's
through the 1970's quite accurately depict a city in the grips of
physical blight, rampant crime, social tensions, and fiscal insolvency. William Friedkin's *The French Connection* (1971) traces an international narcotics network through decaying Brooklyn streets; Sidney Lumet's *Serpico* (1973) locates police corruption amid wasted
spaces of infrastructural detritus at the city's edge, Martin Scorsese's
Taxi Driver (1976) portrays Robert DeNiro as a Vietnam War veteran whose mental illness seems to swell in corollary to the movement
of his taxi across New York's gritty streets. Further examples are
numerous.[56]

Given the setting and content of so many of the films that followed Mayor Lindsay's Executive Order, a claim that they solicited
desire may seem counterintuitive. More natural would be the opposite: repulsion and sound condemnation of the blight and vice within the urban contexts depicted. Such a reaction would have been in
keeping with the prevailing cultural sentiment from the preceding
decades about the malignancies of urbanity.[57] Here, it is constructive to recall an argument first forwarded in the first half of this
book, regarding the treatment of urban decay in *What is the City but*

54   Metz theorizes this unattainability as a critic element within the scopic drive. He argues that the
distance required to effectively see an object ne-
cessitates the lack of obtaining the same object.
In this way, Metz associated the scopic drive with
the lack, and therefore, again, with the lure of the
ego-ideal. Metz, 59.

55   Also as recalled in the first part of this book, simultaneous decentralization in Hollywood production
combined with diminishing box-office returns

fueled a movement of young "New Hollywood"
filmmakers who brought to their craft avant-
garde filmic techniques drawn from underground
film and the French New Wave.

56   For several further examples, see James Sanders,
Celluloid Skyline: New York and the Movies (New
York: Knopf, 2003), 366–398.

57   As recalled in Part 1, Lindsay himself discusses
these narratives. See: John V. Lindsay, *The City*
(New York: Norton, 1970), 50–60.

the People?. There, it was suggested that the film simultaneously solicited repulsion and attraction. The abject content was described
as co-mingling with a strange allure emanating from the sophisticated aesthetics of the cinematography, with contributions by industry
tradesman Arthur Ornitz. A related effect has been described in the
preceding analysis of the enticements of authenticity in *Our Vanishing Legacy*. The same might be identified in many of the films produced in New York following Mayor Lindsay's Executive Order 10.
Such desire aligns with what theorist Slavoj Zizek has called the passion for the real.

Like Christian Metz, Slavoj Zizek writes within the system
of psychoanalytic theory developed by Jacques Lacan. But while
Metz's film theory addresses the interrelation between the symbolic
and imaginary stages of subjective development, Zizek's interest is
in the third Lacanian category, the real.[58] The real encompasses all
that is most deeply authentic, yet critically resistant to the linguistic
codification that might integrate it into the life-world. In Zizek's formulation, we live within a social reality that is composed of language
and convention. Beneath this conventional reality is the ultimately
unattainable and unknowable real—a profound authenticity for
which we fruitlessly yearn.[59] We search for this authenticity through
flirtations with the most taboo or extreme categories of experience:
death, war, deviant sexuality, and all manner of the abject. Zizek
writes in the contemporary context, decades after the time period en-
compassed in the present discussion. And yet the theorist's work
sheds some light on the appeal of the blighted conditions depicted in
films like so many enabled by Mayor Lindsay's policies.

Framing the contemporary relevance of his topic, Zizek posits
that the twentieth century is best characterized as a series of traumatic collisions with the real through war, social unrest, and terror-
ism. Hence, like no other era, the past century witnessed the emergence of the real as a culturally formative category. Zizek notes that
the resultant cultural fascination with the real is reflected in mediated representations of traumatic events that present the aestheticized
"effect of the real." The popularity of some of Hollywood and television's most common topics like war, death, Armageddon and natural disasters are all indebted to the subjective yearning to identify
with the profound authenticity of the real. These two points are intricately intertwined. For as the tumult of the twentieth century has
forced us into direct interaction with the real, we cannot integrate it
into our social reality and are tragically destined to sublimate our
desire for the real for its own effect—for the aestheticized portrayal

58   Zizek cites the influence of philosopher Alain Ba-
diou in his thought about the passion for the real.
Slavoj Zizek, *Welcome to the Desert of the Real*
(London: Verso, 2002), 5–6.

59   Slavoj Zizek, *The Sublime Object of Ideology*
(London: Verso, 1989), 3, 47–49.

of the real in media. The appearance of this "effect of the real" initiates a bitter tautology, only making the impulse to identify through
the real more fervent, as its aestheticized effect fails to satiate one's
desire. In sum, Zizek describes the contemporary subject's tortured
yearning for identification with the profoundly authentic within the
context of a contemporary culture that is increasingly divested of
authenticity.[60]

The catalysts that Zizek identifies for the emergence of the
real align compellingly with the social unrest, physical blight, and
simultaneous documentation of those events in media during the
Lindsay Administration. Added to these factors, the rebuilding of
much of the city in a corporate modernist style of architecture that
so many found to be lacking a connection to the past amplified a
sense of inauthenticity amid urban culture. With this, it is possible
to speculate on one source of the strange effects of desire emanating from films depicting New York City's blight during the Lindsay
Administration. Comingling with the fundamental desire-effect of
cinema was a deeper seduction, a desire for a renewed sense of authenticity in urban life—a desire for the real. Prominent among the
films depicting the city's blight that resulted from Executive Order
10 was John Schesinger's *Midnight Cowboy* (1969), another credit of
Arthur Ornitz, the cinematographer of *What Is the City But the People?*.[61] Through a visual analysis of select scenes from *Midnight Cowboy*, the counterintuitive allure of its blighted urban setting may be
unpacked.

Midnight Cowboy

Midnight Cowboy tells the story of Joe Buck (Jon Voight), a
handsome if intellectually immature young man from Texas who
travels to Manhattan with plans of becoming rich as a male prostitute. Buck's plans fail, eventually leaving him penniless and squatting an apartment in a condemned tenement building, along with En-
rico "Ratso" Rizzo (Dustin Hoffman), a crippled Italian-American
New Yorker who aspires to represent Buck in his new vocation. The
narrative follows the two as they struggle to survive. *Midnight Cowboy* is rich in cinematic rhetoric, layers of visual and literary allusion,
and cultural relevance to its time of production. Accordingly, the
film has frequently been the topic of academic discussion through an
array of critical and theoretical lenses.[62] Of particular importance

60   Slavoj Zizek, *Welcome to the Desert of the Real* (London: Verso, 2002), 19–20.
61   While not appearing in the screened credits of *Midnight Cowboy*, Ornitz reportedly worked as cinematographer for screen tests for the film. The credit is listed on his obituary. See "Arthur Ornitz," *The New York Times*, July 16, 1985.
62   Examples span from discussions of *Midnight Cowboy* as a participant in what is now common-ly called the New Hollywood movement (See, for example: Stephen Farber, "End of the Road?" *Film Quarterly*, vol. 23, no. 2, Winter 1969–1970, 3–16) to analyses of the implication of the film to dis-course on sexuality, nationalism, and economic imperialism (See Kevin Floyd, "Closing the (Het-erosexual) Frontier: 'Midnight Cowboy' as Na-tional Allegory," *Science & Society*, vol. 65, no. 1, Spring 2001, 99–130).

for the present argument are scenes in the film documenting Buck and Rizzo's struggles amid urban blight and marginal spaces of the city. Within these scenes New York City's contextual blight is repeatedly converted into vivid and sophisticated cinematic effects, seducing the viewer with aestheticized effects of the real.

In one such scene, the narrative follows Buck and Rizzo to the decaying tenement the two are squatting in the Lower East Side. The scene begins with a shot looking up at the building from below. The red brick and skeletal fire escape of the typical New York City tenement appears draped from a blackened cornice, spilling down to the bottom of the frame (fig. 22). This shot makes the street below feel canyon-like, dwarfed beneath the heavy façade of the vacated building above. The masonry is soiled and crumbling, and a row of windows has been in-filled with brick. Those that remain are covered with exes drawn in tape. These markings provide a vivid piece of realist detail. The exes identify the structure as condemned and prevent the glass from shattering as the surrounding buildings are cleared for urban renewal. They also suggest the haunting visage of a corpse with exed-out eyes, anthropomorphically casting an eviscerated glare to Buck and Rizzo below. Like a corpse, the building appears in a state of decay, and yet solicitous of one's gaze. Thick with temporal sediment, the blighted façade provokes curiosity and imaginative projections of historic urban narratives, as the viewer might subconsciously attempt to reconstruct the events and actions that have left their tracery on the building over time. To the contemporary viewer, or even the viewer in 1969, such narratives must have evoked notions of a more authentic urban lifestyle amid the grit of the bygone industrial city. Such solicitation of imaginative projection, however, is curtailed to the building's surface. While the mind might wander into the spaces within, reflections on the windows prohibit one's view. Despite one's desire to see, the eye cannot occupy nor own these inaccessible interior spaces. The scopic drive is not satiated. What can be seen is thin, nearly cosmetic, and yet it evinces the *effect* of substance, thickness, and temporal depth.

The camera pans down, its motion across the building's surface further elaborating the cinematic delivery of the façade's surficial effect. Finally meeting Buck and Rizzo below, the camera follows as they walk the street (fig. 23). Matching their motion from left to right, the camera reveals a richly patinaed streetscape. The viewer is shown layers of peeling paint of varied colors, effaced signage, plywood, and cardboard in patchwork patterns atop windows, all comingling with remnants of cast-iron ornamentation. The streetscape conveys a sense of bricolage, of real tactility and material assembly. And yet, such appearances of the tactile stand at odds with the absolute thinness of cinematic registration. The street also appears filthy and abject. And yet the cinematic treat-

fig.
22

John Schlesinger. *Midnight Cowboy.* 1969. Frame enlargement.

fig.
23

John Schlesinger. *Midnight Cowboy.* 1969. Frame enlargement.

ment of such filth enrolls the urban context into imagery that is intensely seductive in its aesthetic. Akin to a contemporaneous Robert Rauschenberg canvas, the streetscape appears as a compilation of distressed historic fragments in seemingly purposefully composed disharmony.[63]

Buck and Rizzo turn the corner to move between the side of the tenement and a chain-link fence guarding the adjacent demolition site. Viewing the two from the opposite side of the fence, the chain-link pattern recalls the morbid exes on the building's façade windows. The pattern of exes overlays Buck and Rizzo, the richly textural rough masonry on the tenement's side-wall, and a similarly scaled pattern of trash that has accumulated on the ground (fig. 24). With this, the grain, scale, and absolute resolution of detail captured in the image are nearly didactic in their announcement of cinema's

---

63   Art historian Joshua Shannon has described re-
      newed attention by New York City artists in the
      1960s to the blighted material landscape of the
      post-industrial city. Shannon argues that such re-
      newed attention should be understood in the con-
      text of, and in response to, an increasing sense of
      abstraction attendant to neo-liberal urban devel-
      opment patterns. See: Joshua Shannon, *The Dis-
      appearance of Object: New York and the Rise
      of the Postmodern City* (New Haven: Yale Univer-
      sity Press, 2009). Shannon specifically discuss-
      es Robert Rauschenberg in this regard. Shannon,
      94–148.

capacity to capture the visual effect of reality. The camera pans, creating a vague moire when registering the chain-link on the oblique. Here, the previous bricolage segues to a kind of Op-art. The moire layers on top of Buck, Rizzo, and the lush textural surfaces beyond— titillating the viewer into a heightened level of awareness through the rote documentation of so much visual information (fig. 25). The filmic aesthetic produces an urban scene that appears even more real than that which can be apprehended with the naked eye.

Entering through a door in the tenement's light well made accessible by the surrounding demolition, Buck and Rizzo pass into a dark and decaying stairwell, and then into an equally decaying apartment, now likely a designed set. The preceding sequence is remarkable: for its attention to realist accuracy, for the urban blight depicted, and for the way in which both are enrolled into seductive cinematic effect. The blight is made semantic, as in the recurrent trope of the exes. Moreover, it is made affective, setting a tone or mood for the drama that is both repellant and sublime. Despite the abject conditions depicted, despite overarching themes of death and decay, the viewer is drawn to these cinematic images evincing narratives of urban authenticity and the rich aesthetic realm of material urban detritus.

In one further example, later in the film, we watch Buck and Rizzo walking along another downtown street at night. Lacking streetlights, the scene is poorly lit. Blackened windows suggest that the surrounding buildings are mostly vacant. Details of decrepit storefronts are only barely visible, and the horizontal surfaces are thinly coated with snow, reflecting what light is provided in the scene, and creating a rich atmospheric contrast between the darkened building façades and the luminous snow-covering (fig. 26). The scene recalls the mood of a black and white film noir, mysterious and seductive in its atmospheric effect. With that, allusions again to a seemingly authentic bygone urbanism of the early 20th century.

fig.
24

John Schlesinger. *Midnight Cowboy.* 1969. Frame enlargement.

John Schlesinger. *Midnight Cowboy.* 1969. Frame enlargement.

fig.
25

John Schlesinger. *Midnight Cowboy.* 1969. Frame enlargement.

fig.
26

We follow Buck and Rizzo along the street with a tracking shot that begins close to the pair and zooms out as the two move along the sidewalk. As they walk, passing in and out of shadow and steam, they disappear and reappear as a gently illuminated moving profile. We hear coughing, a barking dog, and the engine of a passing motorcycle—auditory details that add to the scene's realist accuracy and atmospheric effect.

Reaching the steps of a residential building, Buck and Rizzo find a florescent orange arrow pointing to the door, sharply contrasting the muted tonal range of the surroundings (fig. 27). Passing inside, the two find themselves surrounded by a raging psychedelic loft party. Artists, hippies, filmmakers, and beatniks mingle with costumed guests and apparent high-society New Yorkers. Highly stylized filmic montages and abstractions, recalling then-contemporary experimental cinema, are projected on the walls (fig. 28). Here, the decaying urban neighborhood outside serves as a signifier, like the bright orange arrow, to the hip lifestyles nested within. The carefully shot city street and atmospheric lighting transforms the decrepit streetscape into a romanticized aesthetic for association with a cool urban subculture. Inside the loft, artists and filmmakers—exactly those

John Schlesinger. *Midnight Cowboy.* 1969. Frame enlargement.

who would soon prove so instrumental in making the aesthetics of urban blight hip—are depicted doing exactly that.[64]

The collusion of the abject and the seductively aesthetic throughout *Midnight Cowboy* was noted by film critics at the time. David Denby labeled *Midnight Cowboy's* style "chic brutality"; and the city in which it was set an oxymoronic "brilliant decaying city."[65] Striking a similarly ambivalent tone, *The New York Times* critic Vincent Canby wrote that the film was "slick and brutal (but not brutalizing)." Canby went on to note that "its style is oddly romantic and at variance with the laconic material," and that "movies of this *type* . . . automatically celebrate everything they touch."[66] Canby's description of *Midnight Cowboy* as a *type* is apt, as the film's depiction of New York's blight is akin to those in so many productions set in

John Schlesinger. *Midnight Cowboy.* 1969. Frame enlargement.

---

64   This scene advertises the appropriation of such decaying neighborhoods by artists, a phenomenon that was already occurring at the time. See: Sharon Zukin, *Loft Living: Culture and Capital in Urban Change* (New Brunswick: Rutgers University Press, 1982). Further, by romanticizing this effect for a broad media audience, the film foreshadows the adoption of the aesthetics of urban blight by the middle class—an action that was borne out in the process of gentrification in lower Manhattan that continues to this day.

65   Denby, David, *Film Quarterly,* vol. 23, no. 1 (Autumn, 1969), 20–22.

66   *The New York Times,* May 26, 1969. Emphasis added.

the city at the time. Like *Midnight Cowboy, Our Vanishing Legacy,* and scenes in *What Is the City But the People?*, the urban contexts in these films solicit a strange desire for urban authenticity, for a Lacanian sense of the real. As Slavoj Zizek cautions, these cinematic artifacts only present the semblance of the real, making the cultural yearning for true authenticity all the more fervent. Compounding this effect at the time was the city's preservation of historic and often blighted neighborhoods through special district zoning policies. Like the films often produced in the very same neighborhoods, many of these policies preserved areas in the city as celluloid-thin impressions that powerfully seduced an urban public yearning for authenticity. Such an assertion is affirmed through an analysis of one of the Urban Design Group's special district zoning policies.

Scenography and Desire

The collection of special district zoning policies drafted by Lindsay's Urban Design Group is diverse, addressing a range of issues from local economic activity to the extension of incentive zoning. Recurrent in many of these documents is an interest in protecting the consistency of the visual character of the neighborhoods addressed. Often described in special district zoning as the qualities through which neighborhoods best communicate their historic character to the public, the preservation of these outward aesthetics implicates a scenographic experience that resonates deeply with the representations of historic New York City neighborhoods in media productions from the time. Like the cinematic registrations of urban blight in *Midnight Cowboy*, such scenographic experiences enabled by special district zoning policies entice the viewing subject with flirtations of urban authenticity. The Urban Design Group's work on Little Italy is a compelling example.

The Little Italy special district zoning was drafted in 1976, when the Planning Commission had passed into the leadership of Victor Marrero, and the Urban Design Group into that of Lindsay appointee, Raquel Ramati. While drafted after Lindsay's tenure, the document draws deeply on the legacy of planning and urban design during the former mayor's administration. The Little Italy Special District included the area centered around the commercial activity on Mulberry Street, bound by Bleeker Street on the north, Bowery on the east, Canal on the south and Lafayette on the west. The document channeled the densest development to Houston Street, and directed industrial activity to Bowery while preserving the bulk and aesthetic character of the residential and commercial core around Mulberry Street (fig. 29).

In the document, the aging tenements and storefronts of Little Italy, which likely would have been viewed as blight through previous planning paradigms, were valorized and deemed worthy of preservation. While similar special district zoning laws are now relatively common, at the time the resolution was extraordinary. By way of contrast, in the 19th century the social activist and journalist Jacob Riis famously produced a series of photographs and editorials meant to expose the atrocities of tenement life in Mulberry Bend, an area that was just two blocks south of the portion of Mulberry Street that the Urban Design Group sought to preserve in 1976. Public outrage over the living conditions exposed in Riis's work led to the destruction of Mulberry Bend, and the tenement became an icon for all that was wrong with the fevered and crowded development of the quickly expanding industrial city. Riis's work is commonly sited as a contributor to the adoption of New York City's first comprehensive zoning document in 1916.[67] The 1916 resolution imposed light and air requirements for further development in order to maintain publicly accepted standards of humanity and sanitation.

By 1976, a radical revision of the values embodied in city planning seems to have been at hand, as was a sea-change in the associations conjured by the tenement neighborhoods. The Little

II

Chapter

2

Part

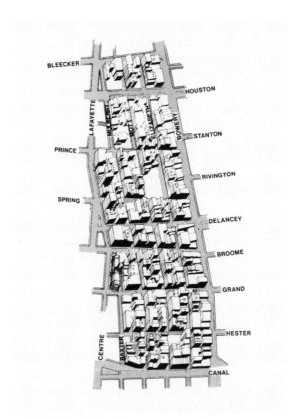

fig.
29

Little Italy Special District Axonometric. Urban Design Group, 1976.

67   Page, 73–84.

Italy Special District document explains that the Urban Design Group sought to "preserve the valued elements . . . in a unified, coherent fashion," and to "permit rehabilitation and new development consistent with the residential character and scale of the existing buildings in the area."[68] The document goes on to state that the narrow streets defined by tenements "perform an unusual function, serving as a stage . . . where children play under their mother's watchful eyes peering at them from apartment windows above, and where friends meet for conversation." The Urban Design Group's descriptions are revealing. The tenements, once synonymous with notions of inhumane living conditions, were now valued for their visual character and for the spectatorial relationships they structure (fig. 30-31). The streetwall defined by the tenement buildings was understood as a scenographic backdrop against which urban life ensued. City planning, once implicitly defining the urban subject as a biological entity whose basic requirements of light and air needed to be satisfied, now understood that subject through his or her visual experience of the city and the associations that such an experience conjured.

These ideas are clarified through a reading of the document's regulations for the development and preservation of Mulberry Street. Assessing Mulberry, the Urban Design Group noted, "Physically the area is characterized by a consistent *visual image* of storefronts and their graphic signs as well as buildings of historical significance."[69] It was this visual image of the Mulberry street-wall that the special district zoning policy targeted for preservation, ossifying the aesthetic of the street's old-law tenement buildings and storefronts through code (fig. 32). The heights of new buildings were limited to seven stories in order to appear contextual to the surrounding tenements, and the street-wall materials were restricted to masonry and glass, with a mandatory maximum of 25 percent glazing. Particular attention was granted the first story storefronts. There, specific glazing, cornice line, and signage requirements were all implemented in order to make new buildings contextual with their surroundings and "insure pedestrian visual continuity along the street."[70] It was this pedestrian, a strolling player within the urban scene, with whom the Urban Design Group was most concerned. Accordingly, the document required the closing of Mulberry Street on summer weekends, creating a pedestrian mall. At these times, pedestrians were allowed to occupy the narrow expanse of Mulberry with adequate distance from the streetwall to fully apprehend the visual impression afforded, taking in what the Urban Design Group called the "old world charms" of the neighborhood.

68   Urban Design Group, *Little Italy Special District* (New York: New York City Planning Commission, 1976), 5.

69   Ibid., 28. Emphasis added.
70   Ibid., 24.

Images from *Little Italy Special District*. Urban Design Group, 1976.

How might one characterize the experience of this strolling pedestrian? In light of the historical adjacency to renewed media production in the city, comparisons to a camera seem apt. Registering the aesthetic impression of the Mulberry Street façades—rife with nostalgic solicitations for the industrial metropolis, and gritty urban patina evincing effects of authenticity—the peripatetic urban subject was a kind of embodied tracking shot. In part a visitation of the 19th century flaneur, in this instance the pleasures of flaneury would be tinged with dissatisfaction. Mulberry Street, now a paper-thin visual impression, offered only a semblance, an aestheticized portrayal of urban

Images from *Little Italy Special District*. Urban Design Group, 1976.

authenticity. Frustratingly unattainable were the spaces beyond the building façades and the bygone urban lifestyles they housed. Mere semblances, like the mediated image, these environments render inaccessible exactly their apparent offerings, making the urban subject's passions only more fervent, more tautological.

The effects of such passions are multiple and interrelated. This desire fueled box-office sales for gritty urban dramas filmed amid New York's blight. Simultaneously, the real-estate and tourism industries benefitted from renewed interest in New York's historic neighborhoods, as previously blighted locales within city became hip and saleable. In turn, New York itself benefitted, as the city experienced increased revenues from property and income tax alike. Indeed, this system of desire elided these seemingly disparate interests within a single, intertwined, and mutually reinforcing apparatus.

Looking now at the contemporary city, it is clear that so much of New York has been reimaged to scenographic effect. From Soho to the Lower East Side to the South Street Seaport, the preservation of historic appearances has rendered the city as an imagistic *representation* of its own past. These environments entice the contemporary urban subject with semblances of authenticity, soliciting desire for the *real*.[71] This desire has now been fully habituated. Part of the second-nature of the contemporary city, such passions have been repeatedly enforced through decades of media production, the planning and design of the city itself, and the complex apparatus of relationships that intertwine between the two. The following chapter will further explore the inauguration of this second-nature.

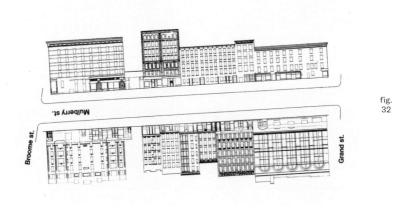

fig. 32

Mulberry Street from *Little Italy Special District*. Urban Design Group, 1976.

71   On this topic, see my own essay: McLain Clutter, "Real High: New York's High Line and the Desire for the Real in Urban Real Estate," *MONU 12* (Spring 2010), 50–55.

Ecology

In October 1970 Gregory Bateson convened a conference in New York City titled "Restructuring the Ecology of a Great City."[72] An academic polymath, Bateson is known in different contexts by varying disciplinary labels: philosopher, anthropologist, biologist, environmentalist, among others. Bateson is often associated with the emergence of cybernetics, an intellectual movement that conceptualized the systemic interactions between objects of study in varying scientific concentrations. The constraints of such systems of interaction, the amount of entropy within these systems, and the feedback-loops that inflect their behaviors are all of critical importance to cybernetic thought.[73] Bateson's contributions emphasized the way in which research methodologies within discrete disciplines might be interrelated; their objects of study re-conceptualized within an expanded epistemology comprising complex processes that span conventionalized disciplinary silos. This approach is most evident in his work developing systems of thought that move discursively between the social and natural sciences.

"Restructuring the Ecology of a Great City" was hosted by the Wenner-Gren Foundation, a philanthropic organization with which Bateson had previously collaborated that funded anthropological research.[74] The event was conceived in conversation between Bateson and Jaquelin Robertson, an architect, original member of Mayor Lindsay's Urban Design Group, and chair of Lindsay's Office of Midtown

III

Chapter

2

Part

72   The late 1960s and early 1970s was a watershed moment for the environmental end ecological movement in the United States. Factors including global ecological disasters and the publication of NASA satellite imagery of the globe created a heightened level of awareness of the planet's ecology among the general public. The year of Bateson's conference, 1970, was also the year of the first celebration of Earth Day. In New York City, Mayor Lindsay shut down Fifth Avenue and granted access to Central Park for Earth Day celebrations.
In architectural discourse, ideas about ecology were also newly resonant during this time. The term "environmental design" came into academic use, signaling both a heightened level of ecological consciousness, and a new heterogeneity of design considerations in architecture. Also notably, Reyner Banham would publish his seminal *Los Angeles: The Architecture of Four Ecologies* in 1971. Banham's book liberalizes the use of the term ecology. He discusses the architecture of Los Angeles, not in terms of individual buildings and monuments, but in terms of relationships to the flows and cultures of four "ecologies" he identified in the city's context: Surfurbia, Foothills, The Plains of Id, and Autopia. See Reyner Banham, *Los Angeles: The Architecture of Four Ecologies* (London: A. Lane, 1971).

73   Bateson was among a small group of scholars who attended a group of conferences at the Josiah Macy Jr. Foundation in New York between 1941

and 1960, called the Macy Conferences, which is often credited as the intellectual crucible out of which cybernetic thought emerged.

74   The final list of attendees at "Restructuring the Ecology of a Great City", beyond Gregory Bateson were as follows: Catherine Bateson, a cultural anthropologist who was also Gregory Bateson's daughter; Warren Brody, a psychiatrist and prominent cybernetics thinker; Frank Gillette, a media artist; Kenneth Norris of the Oceanic Institute, Hawaii; Taylor A. Pryor of the Oceanic Institute, Hawaii; Roy A. Rappaport, a prominent anthropologist from the University of Michigan; Jaquelin Robertson; Albert E. Scheflen, from the Bronx State Hospital; Lawrence Slobodkin from the State University of New York, Stony Brook; Jerome Kretchmer of the Environmental Protection Administration of the City of New York; Conrad Simon, Deputy Commissioner of Air Resources for the Environmental Protection Administration; Fred Webre, Deputy General Counsel for the Environmental Protection Coalition; and Fred Kent, who was then the Executive Director of the Environmental Action Coalition. Kent is also known for his association with William H. Whyte at the Project for Public Spaces. Others whose names were circulated as possible attendees included the architect Christopher Alexander and the sociologist Richard Sennett. Memo, MS 98, Box 39, Gregory Bateson Papers, University of California at Santa Cruz Special Collections and Archives.

Planning and Development.[75] In correspondence with the Wenner-Gren Foundation, Bateson noted that the purpose of the conference was to introduce New York City planners to ecological theory.[76] As relayed by Bateson, Robertson claimed that New York City's Planning Commission had "not had the benefit of ecological thinking" in the methods and substance of its work.[77] This assertion is noteworthy in that it contradicts substantial evidence to the contrary.

Ecology, as it is most colloquially understood to indicate the study of the interactions between systems in the "natural" environment, was doubtlessly present in the Lindsay era Planning Commission's practices. The 1969 *Plan For New York City* included a section titled "Environmental Systems" in which the text discussed natural resources, waste disposal, and issues stemming from environmental pollution within the city.[78] The section's emphasis on the systemic interrelation between these topics is very clearly influenced by ecological theory from the time.[79] More crucial to the present discussion is a more broadly cast conceptualization of ecology that is tacitly present throughout the *Plan for New York City* and *What Is the City But the People?*. The anthropomorphic descriptions of the city and the celebration of the quasi-organic interactions within urban density in these documents—both discussed in Part 1 of this book—color New York as a fundamentally ecological entity. Within these documents, the city is repeatedly described as a complex interrelation between systems of population, economy, infrastructure, and more. Even the Commission's use of media to delivery planning policy can be understood in ecological terms. By using media to effect the city *through* the people, the Commission put into relation systems of media production, the subjectivities of the populace, and the material systems of the city as such. Given such clear evidence of broad ecological thinking within the offices of Lindsay's Administration, it is difficult to accept Robertson's assertion as anything but disingenuous. In fact, it seems more likely that Bateson's counsel was sought because he championed a specific understanding of ecology that

75 As noted in the first part of this book, Robertson was also one of the original members of Mayor Lindsay's Urban Design Group.

76 Gregory Bateson letter to Lita Osmundson, Director of Research, Wenner-Gren Foundation, April 20, 1970, MS 98, Box 39, Gregory Bateson Papers, University of California at Santa Cruz Special Collections and Archives.

77 Ibid.

78 This section begins "The air, land and water which are the physical make-up of the City, the fresh water from the uplands, the flow of the rivers, the tides of the sea and the winds of the weather all combine to provide the City with its environmental resources. Each element functions as a subsystem in the total environmental system and is closely related to the other two. In the past, each subsystem has been managed separately." The quote, and the admonition ending the passage,

clearly indicates ecological thought in the insistence on the systemic interrelationships between the discrete environmental entities listed.

79 To name just one further example of ecological thinking in Lindsay's Administration, in 1968, the city's Department of Housing and Urban Development commissioned a report from the landscape architect Lawrence Halprin titled *New York, New York: a study of the quality, character, and meaning of open space in urban design*. Halprin is a noteworthy figure for his ecological methods in landscape design, both in terms of the interrelation of environmental systems, and in terms of the relationship between human life and environment. For one discussion of Lawrence Halprin's ecological design methods see: Kathleen L. John-Adler, "A Field Guide to Form: Lawrence Halprin's Ecological Engagement with The Sea Ranch," *Landscape Journal*, vol. 31, issue ½ (2012), 53.

aligned with the work of the Planning Commission at the time. A review of the philosopher's central ideas, and his presentation at "Restructuring the Ecology of a Great City," clarifies this assertion.

Related to Bateson's interest in bridging between the natural and social sciences, between the study of the natural world and the study of the development of human culture, is his concept of the "ecology of mind." For Bateson, the ecology of mind describes an economy or systemic motion of information through the interacting psyches of the individuals comprising society. Systems of thought, or what he calls "habits of mind," emerge from this discursive process. For Bateson, a mind is not an individual's brain. Rather, the *mind* is the term used to describe an expanded construct that networks and interconnects the mental processes of each member of a society.[80] Working through the mind, habits of thought endure a kind of evolutionary system through which some are cast-off, while others persist to produce *ideas*.[81] In Bateson's framework, *ideas*, are enduring intellectual constructs that are hosted collectively by a civilization.

Critically, for Bateson ideas are not merely immaterial. Bateson held that ideas are complexly interrelated with the surrounding environment and its systems and processes.[82] To this point, it is instructive to review Bateson's critique of the research methods of the natural sciences—those scientific disciplines whose objects of study are exactly the physical environment. According to Bateson, the natural sciences most often proceed through an epistemology of induction, or by making working hypotheses based on empirical observation that are then tested through further empirical observation of the physical environment or object of study. Induction, Bateson contended, often results in tautological reasoning. To support this claim, he offered a hypothetical story of a young scholar at his doctoral examination answering an inquiry about the "cause and reason why opium puts people to sleep" with the response: "Because there is in it a dormative principle."[83] While the answer is clearly erroneous, and the reasoning tautological, the supposition *could* be sustained through empirical observation. One could validate the hypothesis through continued observation of the erroneous "dormative principle" putting people to sleep, and could even go on to formulate further hypotheses as to how such a dormative principle reacts in differing environmental conditions, or in combination with various other entities. Knowledge about the physical world: the matter of opium,

80   Ibid.
81   Gregory Bateson, *Steps to an Ecology of Mind*
      (Chicago: University of Chicago Press, 1972),
      xxiii-xxvii.
82   In some ways these ideas anticipate more con-
      temporary network theories comprising human
      and non-human actors, such as Actor Network
      Theory, which has been forwarded by Bruno La-
      tour and others. See Bruno Latour, *Reassembling
      the Social: An Introduction to Actor-Network-The-
      ory* (New York: Oxford University Press, 2005).
      Distinct from Actor Network Theory, Bateson's
      ecology of mind addressed only the human and
      non-human elements of the living world, or the
      ecosystem.
83   Ibid., xxvii.

the physiognomy of those subjects ingesting the drug, and the surrounding environmental variations, accrues following erroneous inductive suppositions. Thus, Bateson argued, the habits of thought of the researcher directly influence conventional scientific epistemologies regarding the material environment. What scientists "know" about the material world is complexly intertwined with their habits of thought.

Bateson's critique of induction was not meant to discount the information that may be accrued through empirical observation. To the contrary, that physical objects of study transfer such information, participating in the composition of *minds*, is an important aspect of Bateson's thought.[84] Rather, Bateson's critique was meant to correct the tautologies of exclusive induction. Bateson advocated a method that interrelates inductive and deductive reasoning, and the behavioral affect of the scientist—his or her habits of thought. For Bateson, deductive reasoning entailed the top-down application of scientific laws that are thought to be "fundamental."[85] Significantly, in both the application of "fundamentals" and in Bateson's interest in the habits of thought of the scientist, the idea looms immanent. It is the sustained endurance of an idea that establishes "fundamentals," and it is through an aggregation of ideas that the culture of scientific research is established. Thus, Bateson's particular epistemology makes relational empirical reality, the suppositions and cultural ideas preceding and intermingling with its observation, and the processes and systems of the environment composing what can be empirically observed. Bateson's work now seems prescient, as it resonates with the thought of a broad swath of more contemporary theorists continuing to dismantle the binary of nature and culture: from the importance granted mental ecology by Felix Guattari, to Bruno Latour's repeated insistence on interrelating epistemology and sociology.[86]

With this, it should come as little surprise that in his presentation at "Restructuring the Ecology of a Great City" Bateson was less concerned with the colloquial understanding of ecology and the physical environment as such than with the habits of mind of planners and citizens. Indeed, in describing the conference to its sponsors, Bateson noted:

> The true goals of the conference are two: a) to discover how to think and utter the sorts of thoughts proposed by ecology and systems theory when faced with a problem

84   Jon Goodbun has provided a concise discussion of Bateson's conception of *mind*, and its networked extension between humans and other elements of the ecosystem. See Jon Goodbun, "Gregory Bateson's Ecological Aesthetics—an addendum to Urban Political Ecology," *Field,* vol. 4, iss. 1 (December 2010): 35-46.

85   Gregory Bateson, *Steps to an Ecology of Mind* (Chicago: University of Chicago Press, 1972), xxviii-xxx. The quotation marks around "funda-

mentals" are Bateson's, indicating that he was not suggesting the validity of such fundamentals; rather, he was stressing the important influence of *ideas* that the culture of scientific research held to be fundamental.

86   See: Felix Guattari, *The Three Ecologies* (London: Athlone Press, 2000), 27-105. See also: Bruno Latour, *We Have Never Been Modern* (Cambridge, Mass: Harvard University Press, 1993).

of city planning, and b) to communicate to Mr. Robertson and his staff the ground rules for thinking such thoughts.[87]

As was his common approach in other contexts, the philosopher's remarks at the conference addressed the topic at hand on a structural level, offering few concrete, practical or immediately applicable tactics through which planners or designers might intervene in the city's environment. Instead, Bateson framed his presentation around the broader concepts of flexibility, limits and tolerances in ecological systems. He noted that the goal of any attempt to balance the ecology of a great metropolis would entail "A single system of environment combined with high human civilization in which the flexibility of the civilization shall match that of the environment to create an ongoing complex system, open-ended for slow change of even basic (hard-programmed) characteristics."[88] In other words, a desirable ecology in New York City comprised tangible environmental systems, interrelated with systems of culture or "civilization," such that the totality could sustain or anticipate change, volatility and feedback from either the socio-cultural or environmental milieu. Bateson went on to note:

> . . . I assume that any biological system (e.g., the ecological environment, the human civilization, and the system which is to be the combination of these two) is describable in terms of interlinked variables such that for any given variable there is an upper and a lower threshold of tolerance beyond which discomfort, pathology, and ultimately death must occur.[89]

With this, Bateson began to implicate what he saw as the problems with New York City's urban environment: the city's systems, environmental *and* social, were exploited to such an extent that all flexibility was depleted. Such a depletion of flexibility inevitably leads to crisis. Bateson noted: "The pathologies of our time may broadly be said to be the accumulated results of . . . the eating up of flexibility in response to stresses of one sort or another (especially the stress of population pressure) and the refusal to bear with those by-products of stress (e.g., epidemics and famine) which are the age-old correctives for population excess."[90] In other words, rather that "bearing" with the epidemic and famine that results from ecological stresses like population increase, systems that are linked to human population are taxed, such as food-production systems.

87   Gregory Bateson letter to Lita Osmundson, Director of Research, Wenner-Gren Foundation, April 20, 1970, MS 98, Box 39, Gregory Bateson Papers, University of California at Santa Cruz Special Collections and Archives.

88   Gregory Bateson, "Ecology and Flexibility in Urban Civilization," in *Steps to an Ecology of Mind* (Chicago: University of Chicago Press, 1972), 502.

89   Ibid., 504.

90   Ibid., 505.
      See also: Gregory Bateson, "The Roots of Ecological Crisis," in *Steps to an Ecology of Mind* (Chicago: University of Chicago Press, 1972), 496–501.

In turn, water supply systems might be stressed to sustain the increased food production, and so on until the feedback of systemic overloads spreads deleterious effects across the total ecology. Here, then, Bateson attempted to make clear to those planning the future of New York City their task at hand: the implementation of strategies that might free-up flexibility within a context of accelerating resource depletion, both environmental and social. These ideas were resonant with the facts on the ground. Indeed, the city's infrastructural systems were stretched to their limits, just as social unrest was rampant among the urban public.[91] For Bateson, these two facts were systemically interrelated.

Proceeding from these assumptions, Bateson directed his remarks not to the city's depleted environmental and infrastructural systems, but rather to the stresses of the related systems of culture and society. He noted: "Social flexibility is a resource as precious as oil or titanium and must be budgeted in appropriate ways, to be spent (like fat) upon needed change."[92] For Bateson, to engage issues of social flexibility necessarily entailed engagement with the formation of ideas and habits of thought that constantly and iteratively worked through society. The question, then, was how urban planning might manipulate the ecology of mind. Such a strategy would entail intervention within systems of education and subject formation.[93] Thus, Bateson was prompting planners to consider how their policies might work *through* the psyches of the urban public.

With this in mind, we might reconsider the significance of Bateson's presence at "Restructuring the Ecology of a Great City," and Jaquelin Robertson's thoughts in inviting the scholar to New York. As an academic whose contributions are often associated with the *natural* sciences, Bateson's presence speaks vividly to the affinity of Lindsay's Planning Commission to naturalize the flows and metabolism of the city. As detailed in the preceding chapters, the dissemination of media through the urban populace became one of many such flows within the city-as-second-nature. Certainly, among the liabilities in such a tendency to naturalize is to imply that the city as found is natural—not produced, but emergent by nature. Borrowing Bateson's approach might forgive the Commission such ideological liabilities. By eroding the nature-culture binary, all of "nature" and "culture" are mutually co-determined, non-essentialized, and alike as malleable participants within an expanded field of operation. Thus the ecology of the city-as-second-nature, and the ecology of mind of the city's population are mutually co-determined. Both are produced, and one might operate on the former through the latter, or

91   Part 1 of this volume provides a concise treatment of the simultaneous physical and social urban issues rampant in New York City at the time.

92   Gregory Bateson, "Ecology and Flexibility in Urban Civilization," in *Steps to an Ecology of Mind* (Chicago: University of Chicago Press, 1972), 505.

93   Ibid., 507.

vice-versa. Following this, the 1969 *Plan For New York City, What Is the City But the People?*, and even the media enabled in New York through Mayor Lindsay's Executive Order 10 can all be understood as a means of engagement with Bateson's concept of the ecology of mind. In Batesonian rhetoric, we might understand the critical mass of the Planning Commission's work discussed in this book as an attempt to affect the habits of mind of their audience, thus changing the built environment through the feedback loops that would emerge from the recalibrated mental ecology of the public. Far from introducing the Planning Commission to ecological thinking, Bateson's presence was a postscript validation and elaboration of precisely the Commission's methods of controlling and implementing development in New York City during the Lindsay Administration.[94]

But Bateson's thinking has still more specific resonance with a particular area of planning innovation under Lindsay's Commission, incentive zoning. As recalled in the second chapter of this book, this practice of granting developers floor area ratio bonuses in return for the affordance of public amenity was created to encourage the construction of public plaza space below office towers like the Seagram Building. Incentive zoning was elaborated to new extents during Lindsay's Administration, and was a favorite tactic of the mayor's Urban Design Group. The original UDG, which included Jaquelin Robertson, was particularly instrumental in extending the reach and creative potential of this kind of development control.

While never explicitly referring to incentive zoning, commentary upon the strategy seems embedded in Bateson's remarks at "Restructuring the Ecology of a Great City." He queried:

> Is it important that the right things be done for the right reason? Is it necessary that those who revise and carry out plans should understand the ecological insights which guided the planners? *Or should the original planners put into the very fabric of their plan collateral incentives which will seduce those who come later into carrying out the plan for reasons quite different from those which inspired the plan?* . . . The question is not only ethical in the conventional sense, it is also an ecological question. The means by which one man influences another are a part of the ecology of ideas in their relationship, and part of the larger ecological system within which that relationship exists.[95]

94   Here it is revealing to note that the Greek *oikos*, meaning household, is a root to the German *Ökologie*, meaning the "study of the household of nature," or ecology. *Oikos* is also a root to *oikonomia* (the management of the household), which is related to the English apparatus.

95   Ibid., 512. Emphasis added.

Here, what Bateson calls "collateral incentives" clearly alludes to the practice of incentive zoning. Through the extension of economically rewarding bonuses, developers agree to fund building designs that contribute to a larger urban environment that has been conceived by design. This practice requires that planners and urban designers overtly engage the economics of real-estate development. For Bateson, the understanding of development economics common among planners was an important conceptual surrogate for his own thinking. In several documents regarding the New York conference, he noted that aspects of his ecology might be familiar to planners because they are "related to the older science of economics." [96] Indeed, the flow of capital between economic players, and the interrelated habits of mind of capitalist and consumer alike closely align with Bateson's conceptualization of ecological processes.

Bateson's above remarks from the conference reflect this alignment. By implying that incentive zoning is one means through which "one man influences another," or another's habits and actions, he enrolls the practice in his conception of the ecology of mind. However, his tone regarding such surreptitious manipulations is ultimately ambivalent. Later in his presentation, Bateson spoke to his preference for tactics that more directly address the habits of mind of developers so that they may understand how their actions affect the larger ecology of the city. He concluded his presentation noting: "It will not in the long run pay to 'sell' the plans by superficial *ad hominem* arguments which will conceal or contradict the deeper insight." [97] Thus, rather than implementing policies that achieve ostensibly desirable ends through coercive means, Bateson urged planners to address the city's problems at a more fundamental level. In a sense, Bateson's comments betray his own philosophy. His tacit dismissal of incentive zoning may have underestimated the extent to which the *effects* of this practice might engage the ecology of mind of the city's public. Such an engagement might be catalyzed through the medium of the urban environment itself—though the mental or subjective affect conveyed by the built results of incentive zoning. One of the most celebrated achievements of incentive zoning elaborates this fact, the preservation of the theatres around Times Square.

Times Square Special Zoning District

In 1967, shortly after Mayor Lindsay took office and formed his Urban Design Group, Sam Minskoff and Sons, a major New York City developer, had plans for the site of the old Astor Hotel on the west side of Times Square. The developers had negotiated an

96   Gregory Bateson's letter to Lita Osmundson, Director of Research, Wenner-Gren Foundation, April 20, 1970, MS 98, Box 39, Gregory Bateson Papers, University of California at Santa Cruz Special Collections and Archives.

97   Gregory Bateson, "Ecology and Flexibility in Urban Civilization," in *Steps to an Ecology of Mind* (Chicago: University of Chicago Press, 1972), 513.

informal deal with the previous Planning Commission for a zoning variance allowing the construction of a new office building. The proposed structure would not comply with the zoning envelope setbacks that were typically required to limit density and ensure the affordance of light and air on the street level. Minskoff and Sons were surprised to find that Lindsay's Planning Commission did not feel obliged to honor the informal agreements of the previous administration. Asked to offer an opinion on the variance application for the Minskoff building, Lindsay's Urban Design Group, chaired by Jonathan Barnett, with Jaquelin Robertson and Richard Weinstein as prominent members, quickly realized that the issue was larger than a single developer's plans. At stake was the future of the theatre district.[98]

The theatre district in Times Square emerged in the beginning of the twentieth century, as theatres migrated north from their previous locations around Park Row in Manhattan.[99] As Lynn B. Sagalyn has recounted in her important volume on the developmental politics of Times Square, the district peaked in the late 1920s, as robust theatre activity was allied with the related development of hotels, restaurants, and other buildings housing entertainment programs.[100] During this peak, the theatre district was a vital cultural center for the city and the nation. But by 1960 the area had slipped into a marked state of decline. The emergence of film and then television competed for audiences, and many theatres transitioned first to shows, movies, and then to pornography. Times Square became a haven for crime, prostitution, hustling, and urban blight.[101]

Such was the state of affairs in 1967, when Lindsay's Planning Commission and the Urban Design Group was asked to rule on the zoning variance for the Minskoff and Sons proposal. At that point, not a single new theatre had been constructed in Times Square since the early 1930s.[102] Investigating this trend more closely, the Urban Design Group quickly realized the cause. In the then-contemporary context, the construction of theatres simply did not return the investment required. The Minskoff proposal attested to Time Square's continued development value, but such development was not fiscally sound when theatres were included. With the Minskoff proposal

III

Chapter

2

Part

98   This story is summarized in Jonathan Barnett, *Urban Design as Public Policy* (New York: Architectural Record Books, 1974), 16–26.

99   A brief history of the historic development of Times Square can be found in: Stanley Buder, "Forty-Second Street at the Crossroads: A History of Broadway to Eighth Avenue," in William Kornblum, et al. *West 42ⁿᵈ Street: The Bright Light Zone*, Graduate School and University Center of the City University on New York, unpublished study, 1978, 53–79.

100   Between 1893 and 1927 at least 85 theatres were built within a then-expansive theatre district between 38ᵗʰ and 63ʳᵈ Streets, 6ᵗʰ and 8ᵗʰ Avenues. Activity in this area met its summit between 1927 and 1928, when 264 shows opened in a single season. Later, the district condensed to a more compact footprint centered on Times Square. See Lynn B. Sagalyn, *Times Square Roulette: Remaking the City Icon* (Cambridge: MIT Press, 2001), 33.

101   Ibid., 31–32.

102   Barnett, 18.

the fate of the theatre district seemed clear. Eventually, land parcels housing theatres would be redeveloped as an extension of Midtown's already expansive stock of office buildings. Times Square might then be redeemed from blight, but the theatre district would cease to exist. Approval of the Minskoff proposal would have set precedent for such a transition. Seeing value in the theatre district, perhaps partially due to the preservationist sentiment described in the previous chapter of this book, the Urban Design Group sought to intervene through the establishment of a special district zoning policy that would incentivize the development of new theatres.

The Times Square Special Zoning District was drafted by the Urban Design Group in the latter half of 1967. The policy governed the area between 40th and 57th Streets, 6th and 8th Avenues (fig. 33). Within this area, developers could claim up to a twenty percent floor area ratio bonus for providing a theatre within their projects. As vividly

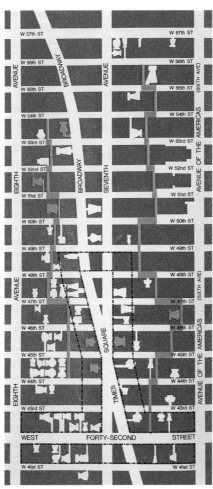

fig.
33

Times Square Special District.

recounted by Jonathan Barnett, the Urban Design Group's experience with Sam Minskoff and Son's was the catalyst for the Special
Zoning District policy.[103] Through an elaborate series of negotia-
tions, the UDG managed to persuade Minskoff that a structure including a new theatre could be profitable on their site, resulting in
the One Astor Plaza building that remains in place to this day (fig. 34).
Barnett's account also begins to elaborate the importance the UDG
granted the Times Square theatre district. He wrote:

> . . . the theatres in the Broadway area had become part
> of a series of interconnected land uses. Restaurants, ho-
> tels, film theatres and shops all benefited from each
> other's presence. Pull out the theatres and you damage
> them all. There was also a system of more *subtle inter-*
> *connections between the theatres and advertising, publish-*
> *ing and the rest of the communications industry,* to say
> nothing of the fact that the presence of the theatres was
> one of the attractions that brought corporate headquar-
> ters to New York City, creating the demand for the office
> buildings that were threatening their existence.[104]

Barnett's seemingly straightforward words resonate with the present
discussion. The theatre district was understood to be a participant
in a network of interconnected urban programs and economic activity. If the theatres were not preserved, the feedback from their absence would reverberate throughout the complex systems in which
they participate—through the subtle and systemic interconnections
with restaurants, hotels and other related activities that had emerged
over time. In other words, the theatres were not only historic venues
for performing arts in New York; they were essential participants in
a vital urban ecology.

Critically, Barnett highlighted the connections between the
city's theatres and the communications, publishing and advertising
industries within this ecological system. Thus, to say nothing of the
cultural messaging delivered through theatrical production itself,
the Urban Design Group understood New York's theatres to be
networked to those industries that comprise the most salient means
of cultural discourse for the city and the nation at large. We might
also understand these industries as those that are most enrolled in
Gregory Bateson's ecology of mind. Advertising, television, cinema, and other communications media are all active participants
in the circulation of ideas, and the Darwinian process through
which some ideas are sustained, that Bateson's work articulates.
Within his comments at "Restructuring the Ecology of a Great City,"
Bateson took note of the relationship between media and flexibility
in social ecology. He stated:

---

103   Barnett, 16.   104   Ibid., 19. Emphasis added.

In our civilization, the exercise of even the physiological body, whose proper function is to maintain the flexibility of many of its variables by pushing them to extreme values, becomes a "spectator sport," and the same is true of the flexibility of social norms. We go to the movies or the courts—or read newspapers—for vicarious experience of exceptional behavior.[105]

While Bateson's remarks seem somewhat dismissive in his characterization of media consumption as "vicarious," it might equally be characterized as a medium of cultural education. In the latter case, spectatorship of "exceptional behavior" in media could be understood as an agent of flexibility in the ecology of mind in practice.

Viewed in this light, the significance of the Urban Design Group's incentive zoning initiative included in the Times Square Special District is much more complex than is immediately apparent. The program engaged the proto-ecology of urban economics, affecting the habits of thought of developers. Simultaneously, the incentives encouraged the development of theatres that were intricately intertwined with an urban ecology of allied programs and

fig. 34

One Astor Plaza. Photograph by McLain Clutter.

105   Gregory Bateson, "Ecology and Flexibility in Urban Civilization," in *Steps to an Ecology of Mind* (Chicago: University of Chicago Press, 1972), 511.

economic activity. Prominent in this vein was the communications industry, including advertising, publishing, and the burgeoning film and television economy in New York that Mayor Lindsay's policies were simultaneously nurturing. The products of these industries were among the most resonant tools for influencing the ecology of mind of New Yorkers, and audiences nation-wide. Lindsay's Planning Commission knew this fact very well. Indeed, it was exactly the communications industry's tactics for tuning audience behavior that the Commission's products were adopting at precisely the same time—in artifacts such as the *Plan For New York City* and *What Is the City But the People?*. Thus, in implementing policies to save the Times Square theatre district, the Urban Design Group was also preserving a critical node with a complex ecological system that engaged and interrelated registers from the economic to the mental. Such an understanding of the role of the theatres in Times Square is made even more vivid by tracing a further endeavor involving several members of Lindsay's Planning Commission.

The City at 42nd Street

On March 16, 1980, Jonathan Barnett, Richard Weinstein, and the architect John Portman appeared together for a video recording of *American Architecture Now,* a series of talk show interviews conducted by the arts advocate and historian Barbaralee Diamonstein at the Parsons School of Design in New York (figs. 35–37).[106] In her introduction, Diamonstein described her guests as "three men whose careers bring together nearly every working reality of urban architecture today." Indeed, the three were present to discuss their interests in projects for New York City that brought to bear Diamonstein's claim. By 1980, Portman had a well-established practice based in Atlanta, and was known for projects that created quasi-urban conditions within elaborate and private interior atrium spaces. Among his completed work at the time were the Renaissance Center in Detroit and the Westin Bonaventure Hotel in Los Angeles, which would soon meet the analysis of Fredric Jameson for its exemplification of the theorist's conceptualization of postmodern space.[107] On her show, Diamonstein interviewed Portman about his proposed Times Square Hotel. Taking advantage of Special District Zoning, the hotel would include a theatre, but had received considerable criticism for its fortress-like stance to the surrounding city.

III

Chapter

2

Part

106   Barbarlee Diamonstein-Spievolgel, *American Architecture Now: Jonathan Barnett, John Portman, and Richard Weinstein*, YouTube video 1:19:35, posted by the Diamonstein-Spielvogel Video Archive in the Duke University Libraries on October 10, 2011.
www.youtube.com/watch?v=5DNTcM0VCaO
American Architecture Now was originally part of a course Diamonstein offered at Parsons on con-

temporary architecture and urbanism and was later developed into a program on A&E television network in 1984, airing interviews with prominent architects such as Peter Eisenman, Jaquelin Robertson, Kevin Roche, Stanley Tigerman, and others.

107   Fredrick Jameson, "Postmodernism, or The Cultural Logic of Late Capitalism," *New Left Review* 146 (July–August 1984), 53–92.

Barbaralee Diamonstein. *American Architecture Now*, 1980. Frame enlargement.

fig.
35

Barnett, who had in 1976 published a book on Portman, titled *The Architect As Developer*, seemed to be present as an apologist for the latter's work, and to verify that Portman's project was in keeping with the vision for Times Square that Barnett was instrumental in establishing in his time at the Urban Design Group. Weinstein, who was introduced as an "ex-psychologist and an architect," was present to discuss his involvement in a massive project called The City at 42nd Street.[108] It is in this project that the Lindsay-era Urban Design Group's vision of Times Square is best condensed.

fig.
36

Barbaralee Diamonstein. *American Architecture Now*, 1980. Frame enlargement.

Weinstein was educated as a psychologist before he became an architect. He received a bachelor's degree in experimental psychology from Brown University in 1954, and a master's degree in clinical psychology from Columbia University in 1955. He later went on to be instrumental in the founding of one of the first environmental psychology departments in the United States, at UCLA, where he was the Dean of the Graduate School of Architecture and Urban Planning from 1985 to 1994.

Barbaralee Diamonstein. *American Architecture Now*, 1980. Frame enlargement.

fig.
37

Even amid the decay of Times Square in the late 1970s, 42nd Street between 7th and 8th Avenues was notable for its blight. Once the single densest locale for entertainment and cultural attractions in the city, the block had become known as the epicenter of the all of Times Square's vices—prostitution, drug trafficking, pornography, and hustling.[109] While the majority of the urban public was ready to concede continued decline, redevelopment interest emerged from the private sector. In 1976, Fred S. Papert, a developer and former President of the Municipal Arts Society, initiated an effort to revive 42nd Street. Papert's first move was to found the non-profit 42nd Street Development Corporation, which was successful in building off-Broadway performing arts venues between Ninth and Eleventh Avenues within a project called Theatre Row.[110] The latter was sited in a relatively intact portion of 42nd Street, especially as compared to the blighted block that crossed Times Square, between 7th and 8th Avenues. But by 1978, Papert had set his sights on developing this most storied and troubled block of 42nd Street with the founding of another non-profit organization, The City at 42nd Street Inc. With generous funding from the Ford Foundation, Papert was joined by former Planning Commission Chair Donald Elliott, who would serve as President of The City at 42nd Street, and Richard Weinstein, who served as a Vice-President and design lead for the project.

Discussing The City at 42nd Street on *American Architecture Now*, Richard Weinstein echoed and elaborated Jonathan Barnett's above treatment of Times Square as an intricate urban ecology. Weinstein explained that the site was the locale of a complex nexus

109   William Kornblum and Vernon Bogg, "The Social Ecology of the Bright Lights District," in William Kornblum, et al. *West 42nd Street: The Bright Light Zone*, Graduate School and University Center

of the City University of New York, unpublished study, 1978, 17–51.

110   Sagalyn, 59.

of interrelated economic, cultural, and material systems. He offered a teleological assessment of the area, beginning with the construction of eight subway lines under Times Square near the turn of the twentieth century. The increased flow of mobility provided by this infrastructure spurred the relocation of the garment industry to the area. Following suit, the entertainment industry moved to Times Square, taking advantage of the broad audience base made newly available by the subway lines. Weinstein claimed that an economic symbiosis then emerged between the success of garment industry and Broadway theatres. Wealthy garment industry businessmen financed theatrical productions, and the success of those productions added capital to the garment industry. This economic interdependency and the population flow through the site enabled by the subway lines sustained Times Square throughout its peak in the first half of the twentieth century.[111]

This balanced urban ecology was later disturbed by cultural, economic and juridical factors. According to Weinstein, the onslaught of prohibition privatized entertainment, as public venues could no longer serve alcohol. In addition, cinema emerged, competing with theatres for audiences. And finally, the Great Depression added to the economic decline in the theatre industry. In Weinstein's assessment, the interaction of all of these factors led to the decline of 42nd Street. Theatres soon transitioned to showing movies and then pornography. The same infrastructural systems that provided accessibility, aiding in Times Square's ascent, then irrigated the declining site with prostitution, the drug trade, and other crimes. This, according to Weinstein, initiated a "negative social ecology" on 42nd Street. The illegal activities on the site interacted and supported one-another, the transient population through Times Square provided a consumer base for drugs and prostitution, and critically the aesthetic effect of the physical decline of the area "suggested society's standards (were) relaxed," working through the mental ecology of the city's citizens. The conditions on 42nd Street reflected systemic failure across the urban ecology.

Nevertheless, Weinstein asserted that 42nd Street retained some "latent strengths." He noted the street's proximity to the economic activity in the central business district, the adjacency of the communications industries, continued presence of the garment industry and flow of population through the site enabled by the infrastructure. These elements needed to be put into sustainable relation

111 Here, Weinstein's thoughts were likely influenced by a report commissioned by the Ford Foundation on the social ecology of Times Square: William Kornblum, et al. *West 42nd Street: The Bright Light Zone*, Graduate School and University Center of the City University of New York, unpublished study, 1978. Within that volume, William Kornblum's and Vernon Bogg's, "The Social Ecology of the Bright Lights District," 17–51, and Stanley Buder's, "Forty-Second Street at the Crossroads: A History of Broadway to Eighth Avenue," 53–79, were likely particularly informative.

with one-another. Thus, what was required to rehabilitate 42ⁿᵈ Street was an insertion that might rebalance the intricate urban ecology, and its interrelated cultural, economic, and material systems. Such was the goal of The City at 42ⁿᵈ Street.

Described by its creators as "the most ambitious and realistic plan ever proposed for the reconstruction of the heart of New York City,"[112] The City at 42ⁿᵈ Street was scaled in proportion to its claims. The development would have spanned roughly between Broadway and 8ᵗʰ Avenue to the east and west, 43ʳᵈ and 40ᵗʰ Streets to the north and south. The complex was billed as "a major entertainment / information / communications center . . . containing theatres, performing arts studios, exhibits, museums, retail shops, multimedia displays and cinemas, restaurants, and indoor gardens conceived and executed by outstanding architects, artists and designers."[113] The City at 42ⁿᵈ Street was designed to include nine theatres. The historic New Amsterdam and Victory Theatres would have been fully restored and the Selwyn, Apollo, and Harris Theatres were to be renovated as performing arts venues. Added to these were an IMAX theatre, an enormous immersive movie theatre in the shape of a cone, and another with frontage on 42ⁿᵈ Street in the shape of a cylinder. The project also contained 500,000 square feet of cultural exhibition space, three high rise office towers, a hotel, approximately 300,000 square feet of retail and restaurant space, and a 2,000,000 square foot "fashion mart" that was intended to provide space for an extension of the garment industry. The entire complex was linked through a series of atrium spaces and walkways elevated above the streets below, channeling through the blocks to the north all the way to 45ᵗʰ Street. Below, The City at 42ⁿᵈ Street would have connected to the 7ᵗʰ and 8ᵗʰ Avenue subway lines, and the elevated walkways stretched to the Port Authority Bus Terminal (figs. 38).[114] Containing cultural amenities, corporate offices, the historic garment industry, hotels, communications, commerce, and a constant flow of people through the complex provided by the interconnected infrastructure, The City at 42ⁿᵈ Street internalized the ingredients of the ecology Barnett and Weinstein described in Times Square. Indeed, the project was a restaging and rebalancing of that ecology in a massive interior urbanism.

As in the Urban Design Group's Times Square Special District zoning, The City at 42ⁿᵈ Street negotiated a complex proto-ecological network of economic incentives and exchanges. The project would have required that the city first assemble the land parcels needed through powers of eminent domain, then leasing the property to The

112   Undated pamphlet title "The City at 42ⁿᵈ Street," Ford Foundation Archives, Grant file # 07900542, on microfilm reel 2433.
113   Ibid.
114   The City at 42ⁿᵈ Street Inc. "The City at 42ⁿᵈ Street: A Proposal for the Restoration and Redevelopment of 42ⁿᵈ Street," January 1980.

City at 42nd Street Inc. Fueling the construction of the theatres and cultural amenities in the project would have been 40 million dollars of federal urban renewal funds, as well as 125 million dollars borrowed by The City at 42nd Street Inc. To borrow the money, The City at 42nd Street Inc. promised as collateral revenues of 5 million dollars annually for the lease of unused developable air rights, which would be transferred to private developers to build the adjoining office towers and fashion mart.[115] The City at 42nd Street Inc. estimated that their project would make a 288 million dollar annual economic impact in New York City through real estate tax, sales tax, income tax, and other sources.[116]

Also like the UDG's Times Square Special District zoning, the economic exchanges making The City at 42nd Street possible were intended to enable a related system of exchanges, what Gregory Bateson may have called the "ecology of mind" of the urban public. This is most evident in the way the design of the complex integrated architecture, urbanism, and media. Under the leadership of Weinstein, The City at 42nd Street hired the New York firm Davis, Brody Bond & Associates, along with former UDG member Jaquelin

fig.
38

The City at 42nd Street.

115   Memorandum from Donald H. Elliott to Robert F.   116   The City at 42nd Street Inc., "The City at 42nd
       Wagner, Jr., January 30, 1980, Ford Foundation   Street: A Proposal for the Restoration and Rede-
       Archives, Grant file # 07900542, on microfilm   velopment of 42nd Street," January 1980, 4.
       reel 2433.
       Major developers such as Olympia and York out
       of Toronto, Helmsley-Spear and the Rockefeller
       Center Inc. had expressed interest in building the
       office towers.

Robertson, as architectural consultants.[117] The designers proposed an intense multi-media environment described as "a high quality, next-generation entertainment medium which makes it possible to reach a selected audience with messages requiring a concentrated attention span beyond the capabilities of conventional media."[118] The IMAX Theatre, a technology not yet a decade old at the time, was intended to feature "high resolution photography and a giant screen to provide a unique trip around the world."[119] The cylindrical theatre would have housed a film titled "Slice of the Apple," which was meant to "simulate the experience of rising from the subterranean depths of New York City up to the top of the tallest skyscrapers."[120] The Cone Theatre would have shown a film portraying "a balloon rider's view of public celebrations in public spaces around the world." Beyond these, the designers promised a 360-degree cinema that would have surrounded audiences with moving images and a television studio for live broadcast of "audience participation shows."[121]

Linking the theatres and cinemas on the top three levels of the complex would have been exhibition spaces, which were frequently punctured by atriums and vertical circulation. The contents were to be sponsored by major corporations with interests in the designated subject matter, such as a proposed energy exhibit that would have been funded by General Electric.[122] Describing these exhibits, the designers of The City at 42nd Street wrote:

> The major corporate exhibits in The City at 42nd Street will be organized around themes of The Individual and The City, with various elements of this two-track

III

Chapter

2

Part

117 Chermayeff and Geismar Associates, also based in New York, were hired as the exhibition designers. Excluding Robertson, this was the identical team responsible for the U.S.A. pavilion at the Osaka World Expo in 1970. The team also included the following: Martin Stone, Vice President of Marketing. Stone was also Director of the Whitney Communication Corporation and Vice President of the Dreyfus Corporation. He had prior been involved in both the New York World's Fair in 1964-54, and the Montreal Expo of 1967; Frederic Papert, Consultant; Regina Espenshade, Deputy Executive Director. Espenshade was an Assistant Director in the U.S. Office of Community Planning and Development, HUD. John C. Hunt, Program Consultant. Hunt had prior been Vice President of the University of Pennsylvania and of the Aspen Institute of Humanistic Studies, as well as Executive Vice President of the Salk Institute for Biological Studies. Hugh Hardy, Hardy Holzman & Pfeiffer Associates, for architectural restoration. Economic Research Associates, Planning and Marketing Consultants. This firm had prior advised Disneyworld and Marriott's Great American Theme Parks. Michael Buckley of Halcyon, Ltd, Retail Consultants; Robert Brannigan and Robert Lorelli of Brannigan-Lorelli Associates, Inc, Theatre Consultants.

118 Undated pamphlet titled "The City at 42nd Street," Ford Foundation Archives, Grant file # 07900542, on microfilm reel 2433.
119 Ibid.
120 Ibid.
121 Ibid.
An additional programmatic idea discussed for The City at 42nd Street was a film archive in the image of the French Film Archive. Discussing this idea in a September 27, 1979 memo, Richard Weinstein wrote to Donald Elliott "At the instigation of The City at 42nd Street, it was suggested that the intellectual resources of Columbia University be joined with the American Cinemateque at the Met to broaden the film program with lectures, etc. That the entity—as yet undefined—approach the unparalleled French archive for source material which could be used by the Met and Columbia, and that a satellite operation be established in The City at 42nd Street. The Chairman of the Board at Columbia is Arthur Krim (United Artists) which is a happy coincidence." Ford Foundation Archives, Grant file # 07900542, on microfilm reel 2433.

122 Letter from Martin Stone to Howard Annin, General Electric Corporation North Eastern Regional Vice President, May 24, 1979. Ford Foundation Archives, Grant file # 07900542, on microfilm reel 2433.

conception being related to each other by suggestive
analogy. By creating these two main lines of force it will
be possible to illuminate the linkages between human
beings and their constructed environment by means of
the systems—energy, information and communication,
in particular—of which both are composed. Being thus
situated in a common context of meaning, each individual exhibit will be enriched and, prism-like, will function as a facet of the whole.[123]

With this, the monumental intentions of the project are clarified.
Having siphoned the urban public from the infrastructural flows
pulsing into the complex from below, The City at 42nd Street would
have enclosed its audience in atria, interiorized urban spaces, surrounded by programmatic pieces reproducing the city outside. Times
Square was thus reconstituted on the interior. The attention of the
newly captured audience was to be sutured to intensive media environments and exhibition spaces emanating messages about New
York City, public space, participation, energy, communication, and
more. Hence, the role of the individual—the citizen—within the interconnected material and immaterial flows of these systems would
have been communicated through didactic media. Each citizen
would have exited the complex with his or her *habits of thought* newly tuned. The revised behaviors of this citizenry would have eventually fed-back into the city's physical systems, aiding in the rebalancing of the total ecology of the city.[124]

In his remarks at *Restructing the Ecology of a Great City*, Gregory Bateson ruminated about how planning might effect the flexibility in urban ecological systems by noting: "But even so, the law is
surely not the appropriate method for stabilizing the fundamental
variables. This should be done by the process of education and character formation—those parts of our social system which are current-
ly *and expectably* undergoing maximum perturbation." [125] Nearly ten
years later, The City at 42nd Street seemed to be designed to answer
Bateson's call. Indeed, the complex was a vast machine for the production of an educated, enlightened, urban subjectivity.

Of course, The City at 42nd Street was never realized. Elliott,
Weinstein and their team assembled a proposal that seemed both ma-
terially and financially feasible, but they ultimately failed to win the

123   Undated pamphlet titled "The City at 42nd Street,"
        Ford Foundation Archives, Grant file # 07900542,
        on microfilm reel 2433.
124   The highly didactic mission of the media and ex-
        hibitions planned for The City at 42nd Street was
        made even more clear in a proposed *Sesame
        Street* exhibit, described in February 22, 1979
        meeting minutes: "All the elements and person-
        alities of the City—all cities—would be present-
        ed to children and their neighbors, friends and
        helpers. They would include the policeman, the

        fireman, the postman, the teacher, the pet store
        owner, etc., etc. It would be an entertaining and
        educational family experience and could be spon-
        sored by any of a broad list of companies." Meet-
        ing minutes, The City at 42nd Street Inc., Ford
        Foundation Archives, Grant file # 07900542, on
        microfilm reel 2433.
125   Gregory Bateson, "Ecology and Flexibility in Ur-
        ban Civilization," in *Steps to an Ecology of Mind*
        (Chicago: University of Chicago Press, 1972), 507.

support of Mayor Ed Koch. Without mayoral consent, the city could not exercise its eminent domain powers, and the land parcels required for The City at 42nd Street could not be assembled.[126] But for the present discussion, the importance of The City at 42nd Street is not diminished by its lack of realization. Rather, the project might be understood as a lens through which to re-conceptualize its site at 42nd Street and Times Square. To this end, one might reconstruct the experience of inhabiting the vast, unbuilt, project.

Arriving at a subterranean station via any of the eight subway lines flowing through Times Square at all hours, one might disembark amid a swarm of tourists and New Yorkers to enter braiding streams of pedestrian circulation set to the sound of street performers and cacophonous echoes of the crowd. Sifting from the flow to board a set of escalators, one might progress upward, as others transfer trains or elsewhere ascend to the surface. Rising through three levels of infrastructure knotting to emerge in the atrium of The City at 42nd Street's main entrance, its air-conditioned environment makes the *atmosphere* itself seem almost material. There, one is surrounded by a reconstituted crowd, arriving from other subway lines, the Port Authority Bus Station, or the street.

Open for four levels above, the atrium's glass ceiling *recreates the sky*, while the curtain-wall provides a view of the pulsing traffic and pedestrians outside, and those passing above 42nd Street via the complex's three levels of elevated walkways. Theatre marquis from across the street and the surrounding mediated exhibition electronics reflect and refract on the curtain-wall, obscuring the distinction between inside and out. The sound of the crowd, still audible, is now mixed with the reverb of distant messages from the exhibitions, which simultaneously pulse retinal impressions. The messages become more vivid as another escalator is boarded, leading to the beginning of the main exhibition space on the second floor, and interior marquis for the Apollo and Selwyn Theatres. There, a view down through the atrium reveals ground level retail stores with consumers moving in and out, and interior and exterior ticket lines lengthening in front of theatres. The crowded floor makes movement a communal task—an incremental wave across the *swarm* in which one is hard pressed to assert individual will, while the surrounding exhibitions evangelize about systemic relationships between the citizen and the collective.

---

126   In his dissent, and only after purportedly proclaiming support for the project previously, Koch portrayed The City at 42nd Street as a theme park in the city. He quipped: "New York cannot and should not compete with Disneyland—that's for Florida. People do not come to midtown Manhattan to take a ride on some machine … We've got to make sure that they have seltzer instead of orange juice." See Michael Goodwin, "Roadblocks for a New Times Sq.," *The New York Times*, June 8, 1980.
Donald Elliott, for his part, has maintained that Koch's actual point of contention with the project was its conception by "Lindsay people." See Sagalyn, 66.

The flow leads across one of the elevated walkways, where the marquis of the Victory Theatre and the pulsing disk of the "Slice of the Apple" can be clearly viewed, advertising its cinematic section through the city—a movement mirroring the present motion through subterranean infrastructure upward. The exhibition effects briefly become more muted as the crowd's motion braids again. Garment industry personnel move towards vertical circulation cores in the fashion mart, office workers move in the opposite direction, consumers and tourists ebb towards the retail and food service. Progressing towards the interior marquis to the Harris and New Amsterdam Theatres, another escalator is boarded, providing views towards the immense Circle Cinema, where images of public spaces around the world are projected upon the wall of a privatized public space.

Funneled into another above-street walkway, the flow of pedestrians becomes more *kinetic*, before discharging on the north side of 42nd Street into a luminous exhibition delivering a mediated message on energy dynamics. Progressing northward, office workers and consumers again enter the swarm, before another above-street walkway is boarded. Tunneling through the next two blocks, still above ground, the crowd slowly thins before finally discharging into John Portman's Times Square Hotel at Broadway and 45th Street (fig. 39-40). There, while capsule elevators visibly sectionalize the infrastructural flows several levels below, one might stand within a voluminous atrium affront an expanse of glass, gazing outward towards the dense crowd of tourists and New Yorkers braiding in motion in Times Square (figs. 41). Marquis, screens, and lights exfoliate mediated messages which shower downward, while their luminance travels through the matter of the atmosphere itself—swirling, dynamic, material, and like in kind to the interrelated masses below.

fig.
39

John Portman's Times Square Hotel. Photograph by McLain Clutter.

John Portman's Times Square Hotel. Photograph by McLain Clutter.

Times Square, as seen from John Portman's Times Square Hotel.
Photograph by McLain Clutter.

Conclusion

This book began with a concession: in a sense, its conclusions are foregone. As so many theorists and cultural critics have noted, contemporary cities are thoroughly imbued with the character of the virtual. Mediated representations are complexly intertwined with the material reality of our cities, our expectations, and memories of urbanism. Moreover, in the paradigm of neoliberal urbanism the marketing and rebranding of the urban image aided by mediated representations most often benefits the interests of capital accumulation. Cities have become centers of spectacular attraction. Neighborhoods that were once home to the dwindling working class have been popularized in media, and gentrified. All of these points have been exhaustively argued well in advance of the current volume.[1]

In adopting the apparatus as an intellectual construct to describe a network of relationships between New York City and its mediated representation, my concessions have been reiterated. Theories of apparatus, like those of spectacle, are totalizing in their critical condemnation. There is no subjective agency in a Foucaultian apparatus—not for the architect, urban planner, filmmaker, urban subject or otherwise. Rather, each subjectivity is produced by, and contributes to, the complex interactions between heterogenous actors, policies, and artifacts composing the apparatus.[2] Similarly, the strictures of the apparatus theory of cinema hold both auteur and audience complicit in the hegemony of the cinematic institution, its

1   See the introduction to this book for a brief review of the discourse around urban spectacle and neo-liberalism, noting the work of David Harvey, Neil Smith, Christine Boyer, and others.

2   Michel Foucault, "The Confession of the Flesh," in *Power/Knowledge: Selected Interviews and Other Writings 1972-1977*, ed. Colin Gordon (New York: Pantheon Books, 1980), 194-198.

ultimate subservience to the economics of media production, and its programming of audience consciousness.³ What more can be concluded? For the urban historian or media scholar, who I hope will number among my audience, the above may suffice. For these readers, the contribution of this book is to vivify a vast web of cultural hegemony that was known prior. But this book also aspires to indicate a trajectory for architects and urban designers. For those responsible for the design of the urban environment, my introductory concession falls short.

Here another brief passage through architectural and urban discourse in New York in the early 1970s is constructive, this time visiting a much more often recalled list of players, and ideas that will be familiar to most architectural audiences. Beginning in 1973, a group of architects and theorists including Peter Eisenman, Kenneth Frampton, Mario Gandelsonas, and Anthony Vidler were consolidating around the new architecture journal, *Oppositions*. The questions and topics filtering through the pages of *Oppositions* are too many and too intricate to reprise here, spanning from semiotics, to industrialization, to formalism; and ranging in format from critical histories to explications of contemporary design, and more. Among the primary goals of the journal was to build a theoretical basis of architectural autonomy—that is, a basis for thinking about architecture as an independent and explicit discipline unto itself and without reference to external utility or valuation. Critically, such autonomy would hold pervasive throughout architecture's engagement with the

3   Christian Metz, *The Imaginary Signifier* (Indianapolis: Indiana University Press, 1977), 7.

city.[4] The editors of *Oppositions* positioned their project as a kind of re-founding of the discipline in the wake of the ostensibly functionalist goals of architectural modernism, a movement that the group was eager to eulogize or redirect.[5]

To varying degrees in different essays within *Oppositions*, architectural autonomy can also be understood as an assertion of a discipline that resists, or is critical of, the surrounding culture. Thus, for example, Peter Eisenman's 1979 exposition of Maison Domino as a self-referential signifying system can be understood as an attempt to internalize architectural meaning in defense from, or critique of, external cultural codes and moirés.[6] In his brief introduction to the *Oppositions Reader*, published in 1998, K. Michael Hays has repositioned the questions of architectural autonomy that filter through *Oppositions*, stating: "One should ask not whether architecture is autonomous, or whether it can willfully be made so, but rather how it can be that the question arises in the first place, what kind of situation allows architecture to worry about itself to this degree."[7] The context provided in this book might provide one response to Hays's prompt. The complex aesthetic, economic, and subjective relationships between media and

4   The ambition of *Oppositions* to consolidate a theory of architectural autonomy has been concisely argued by K. Michael Hays in his 1998 introduction to the *Oppositions Reader*. See K. Michael Hays, "The Oppositions of Autonomy and History," in *Oppositions Reader* (New York: Princeton Architectural Press, 1998), ix-xv. The agency of architectural autonomy vis-à-vis the urban milieu is most evident in the pages of *Oppositions* in translations of essays by Aldo Rossi, and criticism of Rossi's work. See, for example, Rafael Moneo, "Aldo Rossi: The Idea of Architecture and the Modena Cemetery," *Oppositions 5*, (1976): 105-134.

5   See Mario Gandelsonas, "Neo-Functionalism," *Oppositions 5*, (1976): i-ii, and Peter Eisenman, "Post-Functionalism," *Oppositions 6*, (1976): i-iv.

6   Peter Eisenman, "Aspects of Modernism: Maison Domino and the Self-Referential Sign," *Oppositions 15/16* (1979), 118-128. In the pages of *Oppositions*, Eisenman never explicitly cites media

culture and spectacle as the phenomena against which his architectural autonomy was directed. However, decades later in his essay "The Post-Indexical: A Critical Option," he discusses his more recent work in its attempts to communicate to subjects whose interpretive capacities have been fundamentally affected by an inundation of "media, information, and images"—subjects to whom Eisenman believed the close-reading required by his earlier work was no longer possible. One might therefore speculate that the architect's work and thinking in the 1970s attempted to resist, or stand-aside, the subjective states implicated by media culture, while his later work, addressed to a much more developed state of media inundation, attempts to accept and critique the mediated subject. See Peter Eisenman, "The Post-Indexical: A Critical Option," *Hunch 11, Rethinking Representation*, Penelope Dean ed., (2007): 18-25.

7   Hays, ix.

concerns of the built environment in New York developing just as *Oppositions* was being founded provides critical context for the disciplinary insecuri-
ty so evident in the pages of the journal.[8] Indeed,
in the same brief essay for the *Oppositions Reader*,
Hays indicated as much, noting "For what is increasingly the case after the 1950s, as media culture develops into an all-encompassing system, is
the very lack of distinction among media practices, including the design of form and space."[9] Thus,
following the founders of *Oppositions*, one potential response by architects to the apparatus described in this book might be staunch: the fortifi-
cation of the discipline's center as a resistant kernel
untainted by the pervasive culture of spectacle.

The pages of *Oppositions* also contained evidence of a second potential response to the context detailed in this book, if frequently in derisive
citation. Robert Venturi, Denise Scott Brown and
Steven Izenour published their seminal *Learning
From Las Vegas* in 1972, a call for a newly communicative and fundamentally populist architecture
that would borrow from the semiotics of American strip urbanization and media culture.[10] Fred
Koetter awarded the book harsh criticism in his
review, published in *Oppositions* in 1974. In his
dissent, Koetter stressed the necessity to reassert
architecture as an agent of a desired culture, rather than summarily accepting and applying the
logic of popular culture—as if the popular necessarily aligned with what Koetter called "truth."[11]

8   Reinhold Martin has provided a compelling reading of Eisenman's autonomy in his early work as a
move inward, toward the center of the discipline
and in response to media culture. Martin's complexly dialectic analysis argues, however, that the
interest in communication within Eisenman's
work, nevertheless, can be understood as subjective training in the "pattern recognition" required
by the mass media. See Reinhold Martin, *Utopia's
Ghost: Architecture and Postmodernism, Again*
(Minneapolis: University of Minnesota Press,
2010), 49–67.

9   Hays, ix.

10   Robert Venturi, *Denise Scott Brown*, and Steven
Izenour, *Learning From Las Vegas: The Forgotten
Symbolism of Architectural Form* (Cambridge:
MIT Press, 1972).

11   Fred Koetter, "On Robert Venturi, Denise Scott
Brown, and Steven Izenour's *Learning from Las
Vegas*," *Oppositions* 3 (1974): 98–103.

Koetter's cautions aside, if applying the ideas found in *Learning From Las Vegas*, one could be quick to exploit the apparatus described in this book. The design of the built environment could fully accept and anticipate the tropes and formats of its eventual representation, affirming a seamlessness between the material reality of the city and its mediated reverberations, and fully contaminating the disciplinary core of architecture that so many in the *Oppositions* group were eager to protect.

Thus, within *Oppositions* lie two positions that might be applied to the relationships between media and urbanism described in this book—two very opposed positions published within the exact urban and intellectual context described herein. Viewed with the benefit of time, both seem fraught. The merits of architectural autonomy and direct resistance towards consumer culture, respectively, are a subject of debate to this day. That said, it is a small concession to admit that the strategy has done little to inflect the trajectory of neoliberal urbanization and spectacle. And if the ultimate goal of such an autonomy is only disciplinary self-preservation—that is, merely an attempt to retain some modicum of purity without even a dialectic ambition for engagement with urban culture—it seems a bittersweet prize in which the discipline persists without agency. Equally, the summary adoption of media culture and spectacle to renew architecture's communicative capacities is difficult to endorse. In some ways, the urban visitations of the style of post-modernism in architecture, for which Venturi and Scott Brown were immensely influential, pursued this path.[12] And indeed, it is exactly

12   David Harvey, *The Condition of Postmodernity: An Enquiry in to the Origins of Cultural Change* (Oxford: Blackwell, 1989), 39–41, 66–98.

this path that has spurred theorists of neoliberal urbanism to condemn the spectacular restaging of American cities as an agent to the interests of capital. The crucible of activity described in this book suggests a third trajectory.

Indeed, theories of spectacle and apparatus are totalizing. Accepted to the letter, they provide no position from which to intervene. Points of apparent earnestness or agency are quickly subsumed and inverted. For architects, planners and urban designers, such totalizing ends simply cannot be accepted. At risk of willful naiveté, if designers are to engage contemporary urbanism at all, they must engage the city as found.[13] And as found, the entrapments of apparatuses and spectacle grow only more ubiquitous in contemporary urbanism. Thus, strategies for the engagement of such ideological constructs should be compulsory of any design for the city. Such action will require rethinking the ways in which the designer acts.

Exactly because apparatuses and other such devices of hegemonic culture are so voracious in their metabolism, the designer might spread his or her disciplinary territory, multiplying the positions from which he or she operates. In the latter scenario, the constellation of ideas, material environments, media formats and more within the underlying apparatus described in this book amount to points of inflection within a reconstituted field of intervention. Each document, film, urban space, and more becomes a design project through which the urban condition might be affected. Eschewing conventionalized labels of resistance or complicity,

13   Here I knowingly align with the recent charge by Dana Cuff and Roger Sherman to engage the contemporary city as found, working tactically, opportunistically, and pragmatically—"like a virus"—to effect change through the existing processes of urbanization. See Dana Cuff and Roger Sherman, "Introduction," in *Fast-Forward Urbanism: Rethinking Architecture's Engagement with the City*, ed. Dana Cuff and Roger Sherman (New York: Princeton Architectural Press, 2011), 10–33.

engagement with this field might be more subversive and stealthy. The intended results may be less direct, and more systemically proactive—moving through and reorganizing the interrelated and underlying interests, economies and imaginaries composing contemporary urbanism to effect new aesthetic regimes, collectivities, and vectors of subjectification. As did the architects, planners and producers of media described here, one might work on the urban environment *through* its representation, material reality, and the urban subject, alike, conceptualizing each in their complex interrelation to the others.

The above strategy need not amount to the wholesale acceptance and adoption of spectacle culture. To the contrary, mediated representations of urbanism might be rethought as something to be authored, as opposed to received. Such a strategy also need not amount to the foreclosure of architecture or urban design as a discipline. Granted, the most ardent defenders of a purified autonomy would find their house sullied. But an ineffectual autonomy is an empty prize. And certainly, such tactics whither in the complexities of the contemporary urban milieu. Instead, we might broaden the discipline's aesthetic range through the critical appropriation of the communicative and affective qualities of media, allowing such appropriations to tutor traditional aesthetic categories like form and space. In this way, architecture and urban design might be newly significant in its capacities to consolidate an urban public that is now fully habituated to all manner of media.

Acknowledgments

This book began as a master's thesis while I was a student at the Yale School of Architecture, more than eight years ago. Peggy Deamer was my primary advisor and a source of absolutely essential support and insight. I aspire to her clarity of thought and conviction as an architect, theorist, educator, and citizen. Noa Steimatsky was also an enthusiastic advisor. She introduced me to methods of filmic analysis without which this book would not have been possible, and approached my own discipline of architecture with a sense of curiosity and affection that constantly reactivated my interests in the topic. Also at Yale, Dietrich Neuman, Eeva-Liisa Pelkonen, Keller Easterling, Emmanuel Petit, Claire Zimmerman, Robert A. M. Stern, and Edward Mitchell provided valuable comments or support, as well as my classmates, Enrique Ramirez, Molly Wright-Steenson, Federica Vannucchi, and Britt Eversole.

In the years since my time at Yale, this project has slowly persisted through academic appointments at the School of Architecture at the University of Illinois at Chicago, and then at the University of Michigan Taubman College of Architecture and Urban Planning. Both of these institutions have provided valuable intellectual contexts, nourishing my work with ideas, debate, and discussion. For this I must thank a long list of administrators, friends, and colleagues: Monica Ponce de Leon, Robert Somol, Ellie Abrons, Maria Arquero de Alarcon, Craig Borum, Caroline Constant, Judith DeJong, Alexander Eisenschmidt, Adam Fure, Doug Garofalo, Rania Ghosn, Grant Gibson, Geoff Goldberg, James Graham, Andrew Holder, Nahyun Hwang, Farzin

Lofti Jam, El Hadi Jazairy, Perry Kulper, Jimenez Lai, Jesse LeCavalier, Vivian Lee, Claire Lyster, James MacGivillray, Jen Maigret, Malcolm McCullough, John McMorrough, Meredith Miller, Keith Mitnick, Andrew Moddrell, Thom Moran, Catie Newell, Tsz Yan Ng, Kyle Reynolds, Rosalyne Shieh, Anya Sirota, Clark Thenhaus, Geoff Thun, Etienne Turpin, and Kathy Velikov.

Robert Fishman, Claire Zimmerman, Amy Kulper, and Enrique Ramirez read drafts of this book and provided extremely valuable comments, pointing out connections and implications in my own work that I sometimes only dimly recognized. While they were never directly involved in this project, I also thank Julia Czerniak and Mark Linder for being my educators, friends, and mentors for well over ten years. I can scarcely imagine a thought that one of them has not influenced in some way.

Parts of this book were previously published in *Grey Room 35*. For this opportunity, and for the comments they provided, I thank the editors: Karen Beckman, Brandon W. Joseph, Reinhold Martin, Tom McDonough, and Felicity D. Scott. Other parts of this book were previously published in *306090*, Volume 15. For this I thank David L. Hays for the opportunity and his valuable insights.

During my research I was fortunate to have been in contact with several of the figures whose work I discuss. Donald Elliott has been extremely helpful, agreeing to meet with me, and remarkably producing a very rare print of one of the films I analyze in the pages that follow from his closet in New York City. Charles Harbutt and Gordon Hyatt have also been very generous their time. I am further grateful for conversations with Ken Resen and Peter Richards.

The primary materials I discuss in this book hail from archives that are well spread across the country. I have been fortunate to find excellent assistance in accessing material remotely when it was not possible for me to travel. For this I thank Mary Ann Quinn, Archivist at the Rockefeller Archive Center, Sara Blaylock from the University of California, Santa Cruz, and Melissa Quinones at the Yale University Robert B. Haas Family Arts Library Special Collections.

The Graham Foundation for the Advancement of the Fine Arts generously supported this project in the research phase, allowing me to visit sites and archives housing invaluable materials for my work. The University of Michigan Office of Research and the Taubman College of Architecture and Urban Planning also generously funded this project, in both the research and publishing phases.

Lastly, I must thank my family. I have long benefitted from the tireless support of my parents, William R. Clutter and Lynn Campsey-Clutter. My interest in film has been deeply influenced by my brother, W. McMillan Clutter. And perhaps above all, this book would have been completely impossible without the love and support of my wife, Rebekka Kuhn, who along with our sweet boy gives new meaning to all that I do.

Image credits

Chapter II   Desire

fig. 8 –21	p. 137 –145	Gordon Hyatt. Our Vanishing Legacy, 1961. Frame enlargement
fig. 22 –28	p. 153 –156	John Schlesinger. Midnight Cowboy, 1969. Frame enlargement.
fig. 28	p. 156	John Schlesinger. Midnight Cowboy, 1969. Frame enlargement
fig. 29	p. 158	Little Italy Special District Axonometric. Urban Design Group, 1976
fig. 30	p. 160	Images from Little Italy Special District. Urban Design Group, 1976.
fig. 31	p. 160	Images from Little Italy Special District. Urban Design Group, 1976
fig. 32	p. 161	Mulberry Street from Little Italy Special District. Urban Design Group, 1976

Chapter III   Ecology

fig. 33	p. 171	Times Square Special District
fig. 35	p. 175	Barbaralee Diamonstein. *American Architecture Now*, 1980. Frame enlargement
fig. 36	p. 175	Barbaralee Diamonstein. *American Architecture Now*, 1980. Frame enlargement
fig. 37	p. 176	Barbaralee Diamonstein. *American Architecture Now*, 1980. Frame enlargement
fig. 38	p. 179	The City at 42nd Street
fig. 34	p. 173	One Astor Plaza. Photograph by McLain Clutter
fig. 39	p. 183	John Portman's Times Square Hotel. Photograph by McLain Clutter
fig. 40	p. 184	John Portman's Times Square Hotel. Photograph by McLain Clutter
fig. 41	p. 184	Times Square, as seen from John Portman's Times Square Hotel. Photograph by McLain Clutter. © McLain Clutter

Imprint

Concept and Design:
Esther Rieser with
Liv Briechle, Zurich

Editing and Proofreading:
Charlotte Eckler, Grafton,
Massachusetts

DVD production:
Flight 13 Duplication,
Karlsruhe

Lithography, printing,
and binding: DZA Druckerei
zu Altenburg GmbH,
Altenburg

Paper: Munken Lynx 120 g/m^2
Fonts: Times Nr Seven MT Std,
Founders Grotesk

© 2015 McLain Clutter and
Park Books AG, Zurich
© for the texts: the author
© for the images: see image
credits

Park Books AG
Niederdorfstrasse 54
8001 Zurich
Switzerland

www.park-books.com

ISBN 978-3-906027-85-2